HOMO SAPIENS PART VI

EXPLORING THE HUMAN CONDITION: A POETIC EXPLORATION OF SIXTEEN THOUGHT-PROVOKING REFLECTIONS

MAWPHNIANG NAPOLEON

Dear Readers,

I dedicate this book to each and every one of you. Your passion for reading and hunger for knowledge have inspired me to write these pages. I hope that this book brings you joy, enlightenment, and a newfound appreciation for the world around us. Thank you for taking the time to read my words, and I hope they resonate with you in a special way.

Yours truly,

Author

Contents

Foreword

It is our great pleasure to present to you "Homo Sapiens Part VI: Exploring the Human Condition," the latest work from Mawphniang Napoleon. This book is the latest installment in a series of works that delve into the human experience and offer insightful reflections on a wide range of topics.

In this latest volume, readers will be taken on a journey through sixteen thought-provoking themes, including Philanthropic Pursuit: A Journey to Dignity, The Genetic Tapestry: A Journey Through the Code of Life, The Intellectual's Lament: Reflections on Mars Colonization, and The Paradox of Time: A Journey Through Cosmic Sands. Each chapter offers a unique perspective on the complexities of the human experience, inviting readers to explore and contemplate the world around them.

From The Gender Journey: Navigating Complexities, Celebrating Diversity, and Building Inclusion to Mind's Labyrinth: The Power of Thought and Intuition, this book is sure to spark new insights and inspire fresh ideas. Whether you are a seasoned reader of Mawphniang Napoleon's works or are discovering his writing for the first time, we are confident that you will find this latest book to be a compelling and thought-provoking read.

So sit back, get comfortable, and let the words of Mawphniang Napoleon take you on a journey through the human condition.

Acknowledgements

It is with great humility and reverence that we acknowledge the profound influence of the great philosophers who have come before us. From the ancient Greek thinkers to the modern day visionaries, their ideas have shaped our understanding of the world and provided us with a lens through which to view reality. This book is a mere continuation of this timeless intellectual tradition and owes a debt of gratitude to all those who have gone before us. Their wisdom will always guide us as we explore the mysteries of the human experience and strive to make sense of our place in the universe

Prologue

"Welcome to the latest installment in the groundbreaking series by Mawphniang Napoleon, 'Homo Sapiens Part VI: Exploring the Human Condition.' This book invites you on a poetic journey through sixteen thought-provoking reflections on some of the most fundamental and complex aspects of the human experience. From the philanthropic pursuit of dignity to the enigma of the dreamscape, and from the genetic tapestry of life to the realm of beauty and art, this book will take you on a journey of discovery, introspection, and contemplation. Get ready to be challenged, inspired, and transformed as you explore the depths of the human condition in this fascinating and captivating book."

1. Philanthropic Pursuit: A Journey to Dignity

Oh noble pursuit of philanthropy,
A quest for good, a moral epiphany.
A striving to alleviate the plight
Of those in need, a shining light.
The virtue of giving, selflessly,
A noble act, a path to blessedness.
A sacrifice of time and wealth,
To bring about a state of health.
But is it truly selfless, this act of giving?
Or is it a means for the giver to live?
A sense of purpose, a way to find
Meaning in life, to ease the mind.
And what is the true meaning of aid?
To provide for needs, or to persuade
A change in circumstance, a better way
For those in need to live each day.
Perhaps true philanthropy lies not
In the act of giving, but in the thought
Of understanding and empathy,
To strive for a world of equality.
So let us not just give, but strive
To understand and truly thrive
In a world where all can live with dignity
In a state of philanthropic serenity.
But even as we strive for this ideal,
We must also acknowledge the real.

For not all suffering can be alleviated,

And not all needs can be satiated.

It is a constant battle, a never-ending fight,

To make the world a better place, to set things right.

And it is a task that falls to each and every one,

To do our part, to make a difference, t

o make a change, to be a shining star.

For philanthropy is not just about giving,

But about creating a world worth living.

A world where all can live in peace,

A world where all can live with ease.

So let us take up this noble cause,

And strive for a brighter future, without pause.

For in the end, it is not about us,

But about the betterment of all, for all to be blessed.

Let us be philanthropic, let us be kind,

Let us leave behind a world that is refined.

A world where all can live with dignity,

A world where all can live with philanthropy.

So, let us strive for this objective, with all our might, for an eternal light.

And as we journey on this path of philanthropy,

Let us not forget the true essence of charity.

For it is not just about giving away wealth,

But about cultivating compassion, empathy and selfless help.

Let us not forget that true philanthropy,

Is not just about giving but about changing society.

A society where everyone has equal opportunities,

A society where everyone can live with dignity.

Let us strive to create a world where poverty,

Is not a curse but an opportunity.

Where everyone can be empowered,

And given the chance to be a better version of themselves.

For true philanthropy, is not just about giving,

But about creating a world where everyone is living.

A world where love, kindness, and empathy reigns,

A world where we all can live in peace and harmony.

So let us be philanthropic, let us be kind,

Let us strive to make a difference, in the world we find.

A world where all can live with dignity,

A world where all can live with philanthropy.

But as we strive for this ideal,

Let us not forget the importance of humility.

For true philanthropy is not about boasting,

But about serving with a humble and compassionate host.

Let us not seek recognition or glory,

But let our actions speak for themselves, with a story.

For true philanthropy is not about fame,

But about making a positive impact, without any claim.

Let us not be swayed by the opinions of others,

But let our hearts guide us, to help our brothers and sisters.

For true philanthropy is not about following the crowd,

But about standing for what is right, and being proud.

Let us not be limited by our own resources,

But let us use our imagination, to find new courses.

For true philanthropy is not about what we can give,

But about the impact we can make, while we live.

So let us be philanthropic, let us be kind,

Let us strive to make a difference, with a humble mind.

A world where all can live with dignity,

A world where all can live with philanthropy.

Let's commit ourselves to this noble cause,

To create a better world, with compassion and love as the main laws.

For philanthropy is not only a moral duty,

But also a way of living, with love and beauty.

And as we continue on this journey of philanthropy,

Let us not forget the importance of diversity.

For true philanthropy is not about one specific cause,

But about understanding and addressing the needs of all, without pause.

Let us not be blind to the struggles of others,

But let us open our hearts and minds to new brothers and sisters.

For true philanthropy is not about ignoring difference,

But about embracing it, and finding common ground in acceptance.

Let us not be complacent in our actions,

But let us strive to learn, and to improve upon our reactions.

For true philanthropy is not about remaining static,

But about growing and adapting, to be more dynamic.

Let us not be afraid to take risks,

But let us be bold, in the pursuit of philanthropic bliss.

For true philanthropy is not about playing it safe,

But about taking bold steps, to make a lasting impact, with grace.

So let us be philanthropic, let us be kind,

Let us strive to make a difference, with an open mind.

A world where all can live with dignity,

A world where all can live with philanthropy.

Let us strive to create a world of equality,

Where everyone has a chance to be free,

A world where love, kindness, and empathy reigns,

A world where we all can live in peace and harmony,

with philanthropy as the main chains.

And as we continue on this journey of philanthropy,

Let us not forget the importance of community.

For true philanthropy is not just an individual act,

But a collective effort, that requires a pact.

Let us not work in isolation,
But let us come together, in collaboration.
For true philanthropy is not just about one person,
But about a community, working together, to make a difference and lessen the burden.
Let us not overlook the power of local communities,
But let us empower and support them, to create sustainable economies.
For true philanthropy is not about imposing solutions,
But about working together, to find the best resolutions.
Let us not be afraid to ask for help,
But let us be open to partnerships, and to yelp.
For true philanthropy is not about going it alone,
But about creating a strong network, that can make a difference, and atone.
So let us be philanthropic, let us be kind,
Let us strive to make a difference, as a community, bind.
A world where all can live with dignity,
A world where all can live with philanthropy.
Let us strive to create a world of unity,
Where everyone has a chance to be free,
A world where love, kindness, and empathy reigns,
A world where we all can live in peace and harmony,
with philanthropy as the main veins.
And as we continue on this journey of philanthropy,
Let us not forget the importance of sustainability.
For true philanthropy is not just about short term gains,
But about creating long-term change, that sustains.
Let us not focus on Band-Aid solutions,
But let us strive to address the root causes, with resolutions.
For true philanthropy is not just about temporary relief,
But about creating lasting change, that brings peace.
Let us not overlook the importance of education,

But let us strive to empower individuals, with knowledge and liberation.

For true philanthropy is not just about providing aid,

But about creating opportunities, that can never fade.

Let us not be afraid to think outside the box,

But let us be creative, in finding new ways to make a difference, and to rock.

For true philanthropy is not just about following traditional paths,

But about being innovative, and finding new ways to make an impact, that lasts.

So let us be philanthropic, let us be kind,

Let us strive to make a difference, with a sustainable mind.

A world where all can live with dignity,

A world where all can live with philanthropy.

Let us strive to create a world of sustainability,

Where everyone has a chance to be free,

A world where love, kindness, and empathy reigns,

A world where we all can live in peace and harmony,

with philanthropy as the main chains that sustain.

And as we continue on this journey of philanthropy,

Let us not forget the importance of diversity.

For true philanthropy is not just about one specific cause,

But about understanding and addressing the needs of all, without pause.

Let us not be blind to the struggles of others,

But let us open our hearts and minds to new brothers and sisters.

For true philanthropy is not about ignoring difference,

But about embracing it, and finding common ground in acceptance.

Let us not be complacent in our actions,

But let us strive to learn, and to improve upon our reactions.

For true philanthropy is not about remaining static,

But about growing and adapting, to be more dynamic.

Let us not be afraid to take risks,

But let us be bold, in the pursuit of philanthropic bliss.

For true philanthropy is not about playing it safe,

But about taking bold steps, to make a lasting impact, with grace.

So let us be philanthropic, let us be kind,

Let us strive to make a difference, with an open mind.

A world where all can live with dignity,

A world where all can live with philanthropy.

Let us strive to create a world of equality,

Where everyone has a chance to be free,

A world where love, kindness, and empathy reigns,

A world where we all can live in peace and harmony,

with philanthropy as the main chains.

Let us not be content with just making a difference,

But let us strive to make a lasting impact, that persists.

For true philanthropy is not just about temporary relief,

But about creating long-term change, that never leaves.

Let us not forget the importance of education,

But let us strive to empower individuals, with knowledge and liberation.

For true philanthropy is not just about providing aid,

But about creating opportunities, that can never fade.

Let us not overlook the power of local communities,

But let us empower and support them, to create sustainable economies.

For true philanthropy is not about imposing solutions,

But about working together, to find the best resolutions.

Let us not be afraid to ask for help,

But let us be open to partnerships, and to yelp.

For true philanthropy is not about going it alone,

But about creating a strong network, that can make a difference, and atone.

So let us be philanthropic, let us be kind,

Let us strive to make a difference, with a lasting mind.

A world where all can live with dignity,

A world where all can live with philanthropy.

Let us strive to create a world of lasting change,

Where everyone has a chance to be free,

A world where love, kindness, and empathy reigns,

A world where we all can live in peace and harmony,

with philanthropy as the main chains that sustain and maintain.

2. Invisible Battles: The War Against Disease

In the depths of the human body,
A silent war rages on.
Invisible invaders seek to harm,
Their mission to cause disease, anon.
The cells that make us who we are,
Are under constant attack.
The immune system fights with might,
To keep the body on track.
But sometimes, the enemy slips through,
And wreaks its havoc on the host.
Inflaming tissues, ravaging cells,
Leaving the body a ghost.
The pathogens that cause disease,
Are varied and diverse.
Viruses, bacteria, parasites,
Each with its own nefarious curse.
But science and medicine,
Are ever-evolving spheres.
With research and experimentation,
We conquer our fears.
Vaccines and antibiotics,
Are weapons in our armory.
Fighting against the deadly foes,
That threaten our mortality.
But the war is never truly won,
For new threats always arise.

So we must remain vigilant,

And keep our guard up, wise.

For disease is a constant foe,

In the grand scheme of life.

But with knowledge and technology,

We can conquer the strife.

And as we delve deeper into the mysteries

Of the microscopic realm,

We unlock secrets of the human body,

And new ways to heal.

Genetics, epigenetics, and proteomics,

Are the languages of the cells.

Translating the code of life,

For the sake of health and well-being.

The study of disease,

Is a never-ending pursuit.

But with each breakthrough,

We bring hope and refute.

The power of the mind and body,

Is truly astounding.

With the right tools and treatments,

We can overcome bounding.

So let us continue to march forward,

In the fight against disease.

With science as our guide,

We will find the keys to peace.

For the quest for knowledge,

Is a journey without end.

And in the quest for health and healing,

We will always ascend.

But as we progress in our understanding,

We must not forget the plight
Of those who struggle with disease,
And the struggles they must fight.
For many, access to care
Is a luxury they cannot afford.
And the burden of disease
Is a weight they cannot bear.
We must work to bridge the gap,
And ensure that all have access.
To the treatments and therapies
That can bring them progress.
And we must also consider
The impact of our actions.
On the environment and ecosystems
That shape the spread of infections.
For disease is not just a human issue,
But a global one as well.
And as we work to conquer it,
We must also strive to dispel.
The misconceptions and biases
That often fuel its spread.
And work towards a future
Where all have a chance to be well-fed.
So let us continue to delve
Into the mysteries of disease.
With compassion and foresight,
We will find the keys to peace.
But as we march forward,
We must not forget the past.
For the history of disease
Is a story that must be cast.

From the plagues of ancient times
To the pandemics of today,
We must learn from our mistakes
And pave the way.
For the fight against disease
Is not just a battle of the present,
But a war that spans the ages
And a story that's been recounted.
And as we look to the future,
We must also remember the past.
For the lessons of history
Will help us make the right cast.
So let us continue to delve
Into the mysteries of disease.
With compassion, foresight, and history
We will find the keys to peace.
But as we strive for progress,
We must also be mindful of the cost.
For the pursuit of science
Can sometimes be lost.
In the quest for a cure,
We must not forget the ethics.
For the way we treat others
Reflects the morals we have set.
We must ensure that our actions
Are fair and just.
For the benefit of all
And not just a select.
We must also consider
The impact of our research on nature.
For the balance of the ecosystem

Is a delicate measure.

As we march forward,

In the fight against disease.

Let us do so with ethics and empathy,

And make sure that all have a chance to be at peace.

For the quest for knowledge

Is a journey without end.

And in the quest for health and healing,

We must always ascend.

3. The Genetic Tapestry: A Journey Through the Code of Life

In the depths of our cells, a code unseen

Lies the blueprint of our being, the genetic gene

A symphony of nucleotides, a double helix dance

A delicate balance of fate and chance

The language of life, written in A's, C's, G's and T's

Determining our traits, from height to diseases

A tapestry of information, passed down through time

A story of evolution, with every chapter a climb

But the script is not set, for within our genes

Lies the potential for change, a genetic means

To adapt and evolve, to survive and thrive

To unlock the mysteries of life, and the secrets it hides

The study of genetics, a quest for knowledge divine

A journey of discovery, through the code of life's design

From the structure of DNA, to the functions it holds

To the manipulation of genes, and the stories it tells

But with great power, comes great responsibility

For the manipulation of genes, can lead to disparity

A reminder to tread with caution, and to consider the ethics

For the code of life, is a delicate matrix

So let us delve into the depths of our cells

And uncover the secrets of life, the genetic spells

For in the code of our genes, lies the key to our being

And the potential for greatness, in the art of gene-seeing.

But let us not forget, that our genes are not fate
For they interact with the environment, in a delicate state
Nature and nurture, a symbiotic pair
Each influencing the other, in a dance so fair
Our genes may predispose us, to certain traits
But it's the environment that ultimately dictates
Whether those traits will flourish or wane
And it's through this interaction, that we truly gain
A deeper understanding of ourselves and our world
And the role that our genes, truly unfurled
In shaping who we are, and who we will be
And the impact that we have, on humanity
So let us continue to explore, the genetic realm
With curiosity and wonder, at the helm
For in the code of our genes, lies a story untold
A tale of evolution, and the secrets it holds.
The study of gene, a never-ending quest
To unlock the secrets of life, and put our curiosity to rest
For the more we understand, the more we will see
The beauty and complexity, that lies within thee.
But as we delve deeper, into the realm of genes
We must also consider, the societal means
How the knowledge we gain, will be used and applied
And the consequences, that may arise beside
For with the power to manipulate, comes great responsibility
To consider the ethics, and the potential for disparity
Will we use this knowledge, for the betterment of all
Or will it lead to division, and a genetic fall?
It's up to us, as a society and as individuals
To ensure that the power of genetics, is used for the betterment of all
To strive for equity, and to use this knowledge with care

For the code of life, is a precious and rare.
Let us explore the depths of our genes
And unlock the secrets of life, that it means
For in the code of our DNA, lies the key to our being
And the potential for greatness, in the art of gene-seeing.
But as we continue to delve deeper, into the realm of genetics
We must remember, that we are not alone in our quest
For the code of life, is not just unique to us
But shared by all living things, in a universal fuss
From the smallest microbe, to the largest mammal
The code of life, is the great equal.
So let us not forget, the interconnectedness
Of all living things, in this genetic mess
For in understanding our own genes
We understand the code of life, in all its complexity
Let us continue to explore, the genetic realm
With compassion and empathy, at the helm
For in the code of our genes, lies the story of life
And the potential for greatness, in the art of gene-strife.
And as we continue to delve deeper, into the realm of genetics
We must not forget, the power of diversity
For the code of life, is not one-size-fits-all
But a diverse tapestry, that stands tall
Each individual, a unique combination
Of genes and environment, in a delicate equation
And it is this diversity, that makes us strong
That allows for progress, and for life to prolong
But in a world, that often values uniformity
We must strive to embrace diversity, with humility
For in the code of our genes, lies the story of humanity
And the potential for greatness, in the art of gene-diversity

So let us continue to explore, the genetic realm
With an open mind and heart, at the helm
For in the code of our genes, lies the story of life
And the potential for greatness, in the art of gene-strife.
And as we continue to delve deeper, into the realm of genetics
We must also consider, the ethical implications
For the knowledge we gain, has the power to change
The way we view ourselves, and our place in the world and the range
Of possibilities, that now lie before us
As we unlock the secrets, of our genetic corpus
But with this power, comes great responsibility
To use it for the betterment, of all humanity
To strive for equity, and to use this knowledge with care
For the code of life, is a precious and rare.
Let us explore the depths of our genes
And unlock the secrets of life, that it means
For in the code of our DNA, lies the key to our being
And the potential for greatness, in the art of gene-seeing.
So let us continue to unravel the mysteries of genetics
With curiosity and wonder, let us be persistent
For in the code of our genes, lies the story of life
And the potential for greatness, in the art of gene-strife.
And let us not forget, the ethical considerations
As we unlock the secrets, of genetic relations.
As we continue to explore the realm of genetics,
We must also consider the societal effects it brings,
For the knowledge we gain, can have a great impact
On how we view ourselves, and how we act.
It can shape our understanding, of health and disease
And influence our approach, to finding peace
It can change the way we view, diversity and identity

And challenge our ideas, of normality and abnormality.

But with this knowledge, also comes great responsibility

To use it for the betterment, of all humanity

To strive for equity and justice, in all we do

And to consider the ethical implications, as we pursue

The secrets of our genes, and the story they tell

For in the code of our DNA, lies the key to our well-being

And the potential for greatness, in the art of gene-seeing.

As we continue to explore the realm of genetics,

we must also acknowledge the ethical considerations,

that come with the ability to manipulate and alter our genes.

The questions of what is natural, what is acceptable, and what is fair,

are all important to address as we continue to progress in our research and understanding.

We must also consider the potential consequences and implications

of creating genetically modified organisms,

or selectively breeding certain traits,

on not only the individual but also on the greater ecosystem,

and on future generations.

As we unlock the secrets of our genes,

we must also consider how this knowledge will be accessed and applied,

and ensure that it is done so with fairness and equality,

to avoid creating a divide between the "genetically privileged" and the rest.

So let us continue to delve deeper, into the realm of genetics

with a sense of responsibility and ethical consideration,

For in the code of our genes, lies the story of life

and the potential for greatness, in the art of gene-strife.

As we continue to explore the realm of genetics,

we must also remember that it is not only a scientific endeavor,

but one that intersects with society, culture, and politics.

The decisions made regarding genetic research,

and its applications, must be guided by a comprehensive and inclusive approach,

that takes into account the perspectives and needs of different communities,

and addresses the potential impacts on marginalized groups.

We must also consider the potential for misuse and abuse of genetic information,

and the need for robust regulations and oversight,

to protect the rights and autonomy of individuals,

and to prevent the exacerbation of existing inequalities and injustices.

As we continue to unlock the secrets of our genes,

we must also strive for transparency and accountability,

and work towards building a future in which the benefits of genetics research are shared and accessible to all.

As we continue to explore the realm of genetics,

we must also keep in mind the importance of consent and autonomy,

when it comes to genetic research and its applications.

Individuals have the right to make informed choices about their own genetic information and how it is used.

Informed consent, genetic counseling, and education about genetic risks and benefits

are necessary to ensure that individuals can make informed decisions about the use of their genetic information.

As we continue to unlock the secrets of our genes,

we must also strive to protect the privacy and security of genetic information.

The improper use of genetic information can lead to discrimination, stigmatization, and harm.

Therefore, it is important to establish strong legal and ethical frameworks,

to govern the collection, storage, and use of genetic information,

to ensure that individuals' rights are protected and respected.

As we continue to explore the realm of genetics,

we must also consider the potential impact on future generations.

The manipulation of genes and selective breeding,

have the potential to create unintended consequences,

that may not become apparent for many years.

It is important to consider the long-term effects,

of any genetic changes made,

and to ensure that the rights of future generations are protected.

We must also consider the impact of genetic research and its applications,

on the evolution of life on Earth.

The ability to manipulate genes has the potential to drastically alter the course

of evolution,

and it is important to consider the implications of such changes.

As we continue to unlock the secrets of our genes,

we must also strive to act with caution and foresight,

and consider the potential impact on future generations and the planet,

as we shape the course of life through genetics.

So let us continue to delve deeper, into the realm of genetics,

with a sense of long-term responsibility and stewardship,

For in the code of our genes, lies the story of life,

and the potential for greatness, in the art of gene-strife.

As we continue to explore the realm of genetics,

we must also acknowledge that it is a rapidly evolving field,

with new discoveries and technologies emerging all the time.

It is important to stay informed and up-to-date,

about the latest developments and their implications.

We must also consider the potential impact of genetic research on society,

and how it can be used to address some of the most pressing challenges facing

humanity,

such as improving human health, fighting diseases, and addressing

environmental issues.

As we continue to unlock the secrets of our genes,

we must also strive to use this knowledge for the greater good, and to work towards creating a better future for all.

It is important to approach the field of genetics with an open mind,

and to consider the many different perspectives,

that can help us make sense of the complex issues and challenges it presents.

4. The Slumbering Tapestry: Exploring the Secrets of Sleep

In slumber's realm, where dreams do weave

A tapestry of thoughts and schemes

The mind doth roam, in realms beyond

The realm of waking consciousness

The siren song of Morpheus calls

To guide us through the night's repose

And though the body doth lie still

The mind doth journey far and close

But what is sleep, this elusive state

That steals us from the waking day?

A mystery yet to be unlocked

By science, in its steady way

For though we know the brain doth slow

And vital signs do ebb and flow

The reason why we shut our eyes

Remains a riddle yet to know

But one thing is for certain true

This nightly respite is crucial

For without it, we cannot thrive

Our health and well-being would be crucial

So let us close our weary eyes

And drift into the land of nod

For in the realm of slumber deep

The mind and body are refreshed and broad.

But as the night wears on, the brain doth shift

Into a Where slow-wave sleep doth bring repair

To the body, mind, and all the rest.
This phase, known as non-REM sleep,
Is when the body doth release
Hormones that promote growth and repair,
And help to keep us strong and at peace.
And yet, there is another phase
That doth alternate with the rest
REM sleep, where the mind doth roam
In realms of vivid dreams oppressed
This phase, is unique in its nature
For the brain is active and awake
Though the body doth lie motionless
The mind doth stories, create.
But why do we dream, this question still
Remains a mystery to us all
Some say to process emotions
Others say, to remember, recall
But one thing is for certain true
That sleep is vital to our lives
For without it, we cannot function
And our health, it surely thrives
So let us honor this nightly gift
And cherish the slumber we receive
For in the realm of dreams and rest
We find the balance we need to believe.
But alas, for some, sleep does evade
And insomnia doth take hold
A curse that plagues the sleepless mind
And leaves one feeling tired and old
A host of factors can contribute
To this malady that keeps one awake

From stress and anxiety to diet
And an environment that's not conducive to sleep
But fear not, for there are ways to combat
This ailment that doth rob us of rest
From simple lifestyle changes
To therapeutic interventions at best
So let us strive to understand
The complexities of sleep
And work towards a healthy balance
So that our nights can be deep
For sleep is not just a luxury
But a necessity for life
It is the foundation of our well-being
And the key to alleviate strife
So let us honor the slumber,
And the secrets it holds within
For in the realm of dreams and rest
We unlock the mysteries of the mind.
And as we delve deeper into the study
Of this elusive state of mind
We find that there's still so much to uncover
And mysteries yet to find
From the impact of sleep on memory
To the role it plays in disease
The science of sleep is ever-evolving
And promises to bring about peace
So let us continue to explore
The secrets that sleep does keep
For in understanding its complexities
We reap the benefits of deep.
We must also remember,

That sleep is not just for the night
But also for the day,
Naps can be a delightful delight
So let us not take sleep for granted
And give it the respect it's due
For in the realm of slumber,
We find the rejuvenation anew.
And as we lay our heads to rest
And let the dreams take us away
Let us remember the importance
Of this natural state, each day.
Let us strive to create an environment
That is conducive to sleep
Where noise is kept to a minimum
And darkness, the mind doth keep
For a good night's sleep is essential
To our overall well-being
And a lack of it can lead to
A host of health issues, unfeeling
From heart disease to depression
Sleep deprivation can take its toll
So let us make it a priority
And strive for a healthy sleep goal
But as we journey through this life
And explore the mysteries of sleep
Let us remember that it is not just
A physical state, but also emotional and deep
For as we rest and rejuvenate
We also process and heal
The emotions and experiences
That we've had to deal

So let us honor the power of sleep
And all that it can bring
For in the realm of slumber deep
We find the balance and the swing.
And as technology advances,
We must be mindful of its effects
On our sleep, for screens and devices
Can disrupt the circadian reflex
The blue light they emit,
Can trick the brain into thinking it's day
And suppress the production of melatonin
Leading to poor sleep, in every way
So, let us be aware of our usage
And make adjustments, if we must
For a good night's sleep is essential
And our health and well-being, a must
And let us also be mindful,
Of those who do not have access
To a comfortable and safe place
To lay their heads and rest
For sleep is a basic human need
And should be available to all
Let us strive for a world where
Good sleep, is not just a luxury, but call
So, let us honor the power of sleep
And all that it can bring
For in the realm of slumber deep
We find the balance, the peace, and the swing.
And as we journey through this life,
Let us also remember the importance of sleep for children
For their developing brains and bodies,

Require more sleep than that of an adult's
Their growth and development,
Are greatly impacted by the sleep they receive
So let us make sure that the young ones,
Are well-rested and can truly believe
In the power of sleep,
As they grow into adulthood
With healthy sleep habits established,
They'll be able to overcome any conflict
Let us honor the power of sleep
And all that it can bring
For in the realm of slumber deep
We find the balance, the peace, and the swing
Let us strive to understand and appreciate
The complexities of this elusive state
And work towards a healthy balance
For the sake of our health and fate.
As we explore the depths of sleep
And all its mysteries untold
Let us also remember,
The importance of sleep disorders to behold
From insomnia to sleep apnea
There are many conditions to be aware
That can greatly impact the quality of sleep
And lead to health problems, if not repaired
It is important to seek help,
If you suspect a sleep disorder
For with proper diagnosis and treatment
A good night's sleep can be in order
So, let us continue to educate ourselves
On the importance of sleep and the disorders that exist

And work towards improving the overall sleep health
For the betterment of our overall well-being to persist.
Let us strive to create a world where
Good sleep is not just a luxury, but a right
Where everyone has access to
Comfortable and safe place to lay their head at night
The power of sleep
Is undeniable and vast
Let us honor and cherish it
For it is a gift that will forever last.
And as we lay our heads to rest,
And let the dreams take us away
Let us remember the importance
Of this natural state, each day
For sleep is not just about physical rest,
But also mental and emotional healing
It helps us process our thoughts and feelings
And aids in the overall well-being.
But sleep is not just for the individual,
It also affects the society as a whole
A lack of sleep can lead to decreased productivity
And increased accidents on the road
So let us work towards creating a culture
That values and prioritizes sleep
For only then can we truly reap
The benefits it has to keep
In conclusion, let us honor the power of sleep
And strive to understand its complexities
For in the realm of slumber,
We find the balance, the peace, and the tranquility.

5. Enigma of the Dreamscape: Unraveling the Mysteries of Sleep

In slumber's realm, where consciousness wanes,

And fanciful visions dance in our brains,

What mysteries does the dreamscape unveil?

Is it but a neural storm, a tempestuous gale?

Or is it something more, a portal to the soul,

Where repressed desires and secrets are told?

A playground for the mind, a realm of pure creation,

Where the impossible becomes a tangible sensation.

The ancients saw it as a message from the divine,

A glimpse into the future, a cosmic sign.

But science now posits a different view,

That dreams are but the brain's way to process and renew.

Yet still the question persists, what is the meaning,

Of these nocturnal journeys, this mental demeanour in ?

Perhaps the answer eludes us, in this mortal coil,

But one thing is certain, dreams will always be a foil.

A reflection of our being, our hopes and our fears,

A kaleidoscope of emotions, throughout the years.

So let us embrace the dream, in all its wonder and perplexity,

For in its enigmatic depths, lies a boundless creativity.

And as we delve deeper into the abyss,

Of the subconscious mind, where reality is amiss,

We begin to unravel the intricacies of the mind,

And the secrets it holds, that we yet to find.

For in the realm of dreams, there are no bounds,

No limits to the imagination, no rules to be found.

It is a place where the impossible is made real,
And the impossible is made possible with just a feel.
But as we awaken from our slumber,
The dream world fades, like a fading number.
Leaving us with but a fleeting memory,
Of the fantastical world, that once was reality.
But even as we return to the waking world,
The dream still lingers, its secrets yet to unfurl.
For in the realm of dreams, there is much to discover,
And in its depths, lies a wealth of knowledge to uncover.
So let us embrace the dream, in all its beauty and splendor,
For in its enigmatic depths, lies a realm of endless wonder.
And as we continue to explore and ponder,
The intricacies of the dream, we can't help but wonder,
What other secrets does it hold, beyond our understanding,
And how can we unlock its full potential, expanding.
Perhaps in the future, with advancements in technology,
We'll be able to control and manipulate our dream reality,
Manipulating our subconscious to achieve our deepest desire,
And unlock the true power of the dream, like a burning fire.
But with great power, comes great responsibility,
And we must tread with caution, in our quest for lucidity.
For the dream can be a double-edged sword,
And we must be mindful, of the consequences it holds in stored.
So let us continue to explore and ponder,
The dream and its mysteries, as we wander,
Through the realm of slumber, in search of truth and light,
For in the dream, lies the key to unlock the infinite insight.
And as we delve deeper into the realm of dreams,
We can't help but question the nature of what it seems,
Is it simply a product of the brain, a mere hallucination,

Or is it something more, a form of higher communication?
Perhaps the dream is a bridge between worlds,
A connection to the spiritual realm, where secrets unfurls,
Or a portal to the past and future, a glimpse of what is to come,
A way for the universe to communicate, through a cosmic hum.
Whatever the truth may be, one thing is for sure,
The dream is a powerful tool, that we must explore,
For in its depths, lies the key to unlock our true potential,
And a deeper understanding of the world, and our existential.
So let us embrace the dream, in all its wonder and complexity,
And continue to ponder its mysteries, with a sense of humility,
For in the realm of dreams, lies the key to unlock the unknown,
And the path to unlock our true selves, as we continue to grow.
As we journey through the dreamscape, we must be aware
That the dream world is a place where reality is not always fair.
It is a place where our fears and anxieties can manifest,
And our deepest insecurities are put to the test.
But it is also a place of healing and self-discovery,
Where we can confront our demons, and find recovery.
It is a place where we can learn about ourselves,
And gain a deeper understanding of our inner wealth.
The dream world is a place of limitless possibilities,
A place where we can push our boundaries and exceed our abilities.
It is a place where we can tap into our full potential,
And unlock the hidden talents that lie within, essential.
But we must remember, that the dream world is but a reflection,
Of our waking world, and its imperfections.
It is a place where we can learn and grow,
But the true test is how we apply it, as we go.
So let us embrace the dream, in all its splendor and glory,
And use it as a tool to help us live a more meaningful story.

For in the realm of dreams, lies the key to unlock our true selves,

And the path to a better tomorrow, with knowledge, wisdom and wealth.

As we navigate the dreamscape, we must remember,

That the dream world is but a reflection of our mind's endeavor.

It is a place where our thoughts and emotions converge,

And our innermost desires and fears emerge.

But it is also a place of boundless creativity,

Where we can tap into our imagination, and achieve originality.

It is a place where we can let our minds run wild,

And discover new solutions, that seem like a child.

The dream world is a place of inspiration,

A place where we can find motivation,

It is a place where we can explore new possibilities,

And push the boundaries of our creativity, and possibilities.

But we must remember, that the dream world is not always clear,

And that its meaning and purpose may not always be near.

It is a place of mystery, that can be hard to comprehend,

But with an open mind, we can begin to comprehend.

So let us embrace the dream, in all its complexity and intrigue,

And use it as a source of inspiration, to help us be free.

For in the realm of dreams, lies the key to unlock our true potential,

And the path to a more fulfilling life, as we continue to go on with our mental.

As we journey through the dreamscape, we must also consider

The impact of the dream world on our waking life, and how it can further

Affect our mental and physical well-being, and our perspective on reality,

For the dream can shape our thoughts, emotions, and our ability.

Some studies suggest that lucid dreaming, the ability to become aware

And control one's dreams, can have therapeutic benefits and repair

Certain emotional and psychological issues, by allowing one to face

Their fears and traumas in a controlled environment, and find grace.

But on the other hand, chronic nightmares and sleep disorders,

Can have detrimental effects on one's mental and physical border,

Leading to symptoms such as insomnia, anxiety, and depression,

Which highlights the importance of proper dream regulation and attention.

So as we delve deeper into the dream world, let us be mindful

Of the impact it can have on our waking lives, and be kind

To ourselves and others, as we navigate the complexities and wonders,

Of the dream world, and strive towards achieving a balanced and peaceful slumber.

As we journey through the dreamscape, we must also recognize,

That the dream world is not just a personal experience, but a collective one, and recognize

The impact of culture, society, and history on the interpretation,

And understanding of dreams, and the role they play in our daily interactions.

Dreams have been an integral part of human history,

And have been interpreted and revered by cultures and societies,

From ancient civilizations to modern times, and the role they play

In personal, spiritual, and cultural contexts, can not be understated.

Dreams have been used as a source of divination, prophecy, and healing,

And have been depicted in art, literature, and religious beliefs, revealing

The importance and significance of dreams in shaping human understanding,

And the role they play in shaping our sense of self and belonging.

As we continue to explore the dream world, let us be aware,

Of the cultural and historical context and how it shapes our understanding and compare

With different perspectives, and strive to gain a deeper understanding,

Of the role of dreams in shaping human experience, and expanding.

As we journey through the dreamscape, we must also consider

The impact of technology on the dream world, and how it can alter

Our understanding and experience of the dream, and its potential

For both positive and negative effects on our well-being and essential.

With the advancements in technology, we now have the ability

To control and manipulate our dreams through lucid dreaming, and ability

To record and analyze our dreams through devices such as lucid dream induction,

And sleep-tracking apps, providing us with new insights and reduction.

But as we embrace these technological advancements, we must also be aware

Of the potential negative effects, such as the manipulation of the dream, and the repair

Of the natural dream process, and the potential invasion of privacy,

As well as the ethical implications of the manipulation of the dream reality.

So as we journey through the dreamscape, let us be mindful

Of the impact of technology, and strive to use it in a balanced and kind

Manner, to enhance our understanding and experience of the dream world,

And ensure that it serves to improve our well-being and is not unfurled.

As we journey through the dreamscape, we must also contemplate

The connection between the dream world and our waking state,

And how they interact and influence each other, and the implications

For our understanding of consciousness, reality, and imagination.

Some theories propose that the dream world and waking state

Are interconnected and that the dream is a reflection of our waking state,

Others suggest that the dream world is a separate reality,

And that the dream state is a gateway to other dimensions, truly.

Regardless of the specific theory, it is clear that the dream world

And the waking state are intricately connected, and that the dream world

Can provide us with valuable insights and understanding,

Into our thoughts, emotions, and behavior in the waking state, and expanding.

As we continue to explore the dreamscape, let us ponder

The connection between the dream world and the waking state, and wonder

How they interact and influence each other, and how we can use

This understanding to improve our well-being, and not abuse.

As we journey through the dreamscape, we must also consider

The implications of the dream world for our understanding of the human condition, and further

The role that dreams play in shaping our understanding of our place in the world,

And the role that they play in shaping our sense of meaning and purpose, unfurled.

Dreams have the power to transport us to other worlds,

And to reveal to us the deepest aspects of our being, unfurled.

They can provide us with a sense of transcendence, and help us connect

With something greater than ourselves, and reflect on our own existence, we direct.

Dreams can also be a source of inspiration, guiding us on our journey through life,

Providing us with the wisdom and guidance we need to navigate the challenges and strife.

As we journey through the dreamscape, we must also realize

That the dream world is not just a personal experience, but a collective one, and realize

The impact of group dynamics and social interactions on the dream,

And the role that it plays in shaping our understanding and esteem.

Dreams have been known to reflect the collective fears, anxieties, and desires,

Of a group or society, and can provide valuable insight into the inner workings and entire

Of a culture or society, as well as reveal its hidden dynamics and conflicts,

And the role that it plays in shaping our collective understanding and convictions.

Dreams can also serve as a form of social cohesion and communication,

And provide a platform for shared experiences and understanding, and a sensation

Of connection and belonging, and the role that it plays in shaping the collective psyche,

And the role that it plays in shaping our sense of self and community, and empathize.
As we continue to explore the dreamscape, let us be aware
Of the impact of group dynamics and social interactions, and compare
With different perspectives, and strive to gain a deeper understanding,
Of the role of dreams in shaping collective human experience, and expanding.

6. The Intellectual's Lament: Reflections on Mars Colonization

7. Cosmic Echoes: A Journey Through the Grand Scheme

In the grand scheme of things,

All mortals are but fleeting beings,

A mere blip in the cosmic expanse,

A spark in the void, a transient chance.

Eons pass and stars are born,

Civilizations rise and empires torn,

But through it all, one truth remains:

All life is but a fleeting gains.

We strive for power and wealth untold,

But in the end, our fate is old,

We are but dust to dust returned,

And all our grand ambitions spurned.

Yet still we toil and still we strive,

For meaning in this mortal life,

We seek to leave a lasting mark,

To be remembered in the dark.

But in the grand scheme of things,

All our efforts are but fleeting flings,

A drop in the ocean, a grain of sand,

A ripple in the cosmic grand.

So let us not despair or fret,

For though our time is short, we are not done yet,

Let us make the most of every day,

And in the grand scheme, our legacy will stay.

For in this grand scheme of things,

We may be but mere mortals, fleeting beings,

But our actions and our choices,
Can echo through the ages and beyond our voices.
We may not control the grand design,
But we can shape our own destinies, line by line,
We can make a difference, big or small,
And leave a lasting impact, standing tall.
For though we are but mere mortals,
We possess a power that is immortal,
The power of thought, the power of will,
The power to shape our own free will.
So let us not waste this precious time,
For in the grand scheme, it is but a mime,
Let us make the most of every breath,
And leave a legacy of love and death.
For in the grand scheme of things,
We may be but a fleeting fling,
But our actions and our choices,
Will forever sing, in the cosmic symphonies.
In the grand scheme of things,
We are but mere mortals, with our own set of wings,
But let us not forget, that we are also part of something greater,
A cosmic tapestry, woven by a master.
We may not see the full picture,
But that does not mean our purpose is lesser,
For every thread in the tapestry,
Is important, and contributes to its beauty.
So let us live our lives with grace,
And leave behind a meaningful trace,
For in the grand scheme of things,
Our actions and deeds, will forever sing.
As we journey through this mortal coil,

Let us strive to leave a positive foil,

For though we may be but a fleeting fling,

Our legacy will forever ring.

In the grand scheme of things,

We may be but a small part of the cosmic strings,

But let us make the most of every moment,

And leave a lasting impact, that will forever be potent.

In the grand scheme of things,

We are but mere mortals, with our own set of wings,

But let us not limit ourselves to what we see,

For there is so much more, yet to be.

We may not understand the grand plan,

But that does not mean we should take a stand,

Against the mystery and the unknown,

For it is in these moments, that we truly grow.

For in the grand scheme of things,

We are but a small part of a greater being,

A cosmic dance, a symphony,

Where each and every one of us, has a role to play, harmoniously.

So let us embrace the grand scheme,

And all its complexity and grandeur seem,

For in the end, it is not about what we leave behind,

But about how we live, our hearts and minds.

In the grand scheme of things,

We may be but a small part of the cosmic strings,

But let us make our mark, and make it shine,

And leave a legacy of love and light, that will forever entwine.

In the grand scheme of things,

We are but mere mortals, with our own set of wings,

But let us not forget that we are also connected,

To something greater, that is not yet erected.

We may not see the end,

But that doesn't mean our lives should be spent,

Living in fear and uncertainty,

For that is not the way to true serenity.

For in the grand scheme of things,

We are but a small part of a greater being,

A cosmic dance, a symphony,

Where each and every one of us, has a role to play, in harmony.

So let us embrace the grand scheme,

With open hearts and open dreams,

For in the end, it is not about the destination,

But about the journey and the revelation.

In the grand scheme of things,

We may be but a small part of the cosmic strings,

But let us make the most of every moment,

And leave a lasting impact, that will forever be relevant.

In the grand scheme of things,

We are but mere mortals, with our own set of wings,

But we are also a part of something greater,

A cosmic journey, that is worth the risk and the adventure.

In the grand scheme of things,

We are but mere mortals, with our own set of wings,

But let us not be content with just existing,

For life is a journey, worth the persistent pursuing.

We may not know the ultimate truth,

But that does not mean we cannot strive for proof,

Of the beauty and the wonder that surrounds us,

And the purpose that is yet to be discovered.

For in the grand scheme of things,

We are but a small part of a greater being,

A cosmic dance, a symphony,

Where each and every one of us, has a role to play, in unity.

So let us embrace the grand scheme,

With open hearts and open minds,

For in the end, it is not about the destination,

But about the journey and the enlightenment.

In the grand scheme of things,

We may be but a small part of the cosmic strings,

But let us make the most of every moment,

And leave a lasting impact, that will forever be in motion.

In the grand scheme of things,

We are but mere mortals, with our own set of wings,

But we are also a part of something greater,

A cosmic journey, that is worth the exploration and contemplation.

In the grand scheme of things,

We are but mere mortals, with our own set of wings,

But let us not be limited by our fears and doubts,

For we possess the power to break them out.

We may not know the ultimate fate,

But that does not mean we cannot create,

A path for ourselves, a purpose to live,

And to leave behind a legacy that will give.

For in the grand scheme of things,

We are but a small part of a greater being,

A cosmic dance, a symphony,

Where each and every one of us, has a role to play, in harmony.

So let us embrace the grand scheme,

With open hearts and open eyes,

For in the end, it is not about the destination,

But about the journey, the challenges and the prize.

In the grand scheme of things,

We may be but a small part of the cosmic strings,

But let us make the most of every moment,
And leave a lasting impact, that will forever be a testament.
In the grand scheme of things,
We are but mere mortals, with our own set of wings,
But we are also a part of something greater,
A cosmic journey, that is worth the exploration,
the perseverance and the adventure.
In the grand scheme of things,
We are but mere mortals, with our own set of wings,
But let us not be constrained by our limitations,
For we possess the potential for boundless creations.
We may not know the ultimate end,
But that does not mean we cannot transcend,
Beyond our perceived boundaries and limits,
And reach for something greater, that truly commits.
For in the grand scheme of things,
We are but a small part of a greater being,
A cosmic dance, a symphony,
Where each and every one of us, has a role to play, in unity.
So let us embrace the grand scheme,
With open hearts and open souls,
For in the end, it is not about the destination,
But about the journey, the growth and the ultimate goal.
In the grand scheme of things,
We may be but a small part of the cosmic strings,
But let us make the most of every moment,
And leave a lasting impact, that will forever be a monument.
In the grand scheme of things,
We are but mere mortals, with our own set of wings,
But we are also a part of something greater,
A cosmic journey, that is worth the exploration,

the aspiration and the ultimate elevation.

In the grand scheme of things,

We are but mere mortals, with our own set of wings,

But let us not be defined by our mortality,

For we possess the power to transcend and live eternally.

Through our actions, our thoughts and our deeds,

We can leave behind a legacy that truly leads,

And inspire future generations to reach for the stars,

And transcend the boundaries that we perceive as bars.

For in the grand scheme of things,

We are but a small part of a greater being,

A cosmic dance, a symphony,

Where each and every one of us, has a role to play, in harmony.

So let us embrace the grand scheme,

With open hearts and open minds,

For in the end, it is not about the destination,

But about the journey, the challenges, the progress and the grind.

In the grand scheme of things,

We may be but a small part of the cosmic strings,

But let us make the most of every moment,

And leave a lasting impact, that will forever be momentous.

In the grand scheme of things,

We are but mere mortals, with our own set of wings,

But we are also a part of something greater,

A cosmic journey, that is worth the exploration, the aspiration,

the transcendence and the ultimate realization.

8. Fate's Play: The Balance of Destiny and Choice

In the grand scheme of things, fate doth play
A role in our lives, in every single day
Some may argue 'tis predetermined
Others, that we ourselves are the determinant
But what is fate, truly, in its essence
Is it a force that guides our existence
Or is it but a mere perception
Of events that are out of our discretion
Perhaps 'tis a combination of both
A balance of fate and free will troth
For though fate may lay out the path
Our choices still determine the aftermath
But what of those who believe in destiny
That all is predetermined, and cannot be
Changed, altered, or swayed in any way
Is this not a form of fatalism, to sway
One's actions, and thoughts, and beliefs
To a predetermined outcome, a relief
From the responsibility of choice
But at what cost, to silence one's voice
For if fate is set, and cannot be bent
Then what meaning do our actions have, in the end
No room for growth, for change, for progress
A stagnant existence, in which we must confess
We are but mere puppets on a string
Dancing to the tune of fate's wing

But if we take hold of our own reins

We may shape our own destinies, without strains

For fate may guide us, but it does not rule

It is but one aspect of life, a tool

To be used, not to be feared or revered

For in the end, it is our choices that we must cleaver

So let us not be slaves to fate's whims

But rather, let us take control of our own limbs

For in the grand scheme of things, fate doth play

A role in our lives, but it is not the only way.

But what of those who argue for predestination

That all is already set, in a grand revelation

Is this not a form of determinism, to claim

That our fate is already set, and nothing can change

But is it truly so, that all is set in stone

And our actions, mere illusions, on our own

For if fate is predetermined, and cannot be swayed

Then what meaning do our actions truly hold, in this charade

But perhaps, it is not so black and white

For fate and free will, do not always fight

Perhaps it is a balance, of both and more

A dance between fate and the choices we adore

For fate may lay out the path before us

But it is our choices that shape the outcome, thus

For even if fate may be predetermined

Our actions still hold power, and cannot be denied

So let us not be slaves to fate's whims

But rather, let us take control of our own limbs

For in the grand scheme of things, fate doth play

A role in our lives, but it is not the only way.

But yet again, fate may be a mere illusion,

A concept created by our own confusion
For the reality may be that there is no fate,
Just the chaos of life, that we try to contextualize
In the end, it may be that fate is just a perception,
A way for us to make sense of our own reflection
But whether it is predetermined or not,
One thing is certain, our choices, we must have got.
But in this quest for control and power,
We must not forget, that there are also moments of cower
For fate may bring us challenges, and strife
That test our strength, and change our life
But in these moments of adversity,
We must remember, that they are not a curse, but a gift
For they shape us, and make us who we are
And without them, we would not reach far
So let us embrace fate's twists and turns
For they are the fire that makes our souls burn
And though we may not understand its ways
In the end, it is all a part of life's cosmic plays
And as we reach the end of our journey,
We may look back with pride and joy
For we have lived our lives, with grace and bravery
And fate, has played its role, in our own story.
But as we look upon our lives with pride,
We must not forget, that fate is not always on our side
For sometimes it may bring us sorrow and pain
And in those moments, we must not complain
For fate is not just about the good we gain,
But also about the struggles and the strain
That we must endure, to become who we are
And in those moments, we must shine like a star

For fate may guide us, but it is not the end

We are the masters of our own destinies to tend

And as we journey through this grand scheme

We must remember, that fate is not always what it seems

So let us embrace the unknown, with open hearts

For it is in the unknown, that we find our part

In this grand scheme of fate, and free will

And in the end, it is our choices that will thrill.

For the fate of our lives, is in our hands

We are the creators of our own fate, and we must stand,

With courage and strength, to shape our own destiny

For in the end, it is our choices, that will set us free.

But as we journey through this grand scheme,

It is important to remember, that we are not alone

For others may also shape our fate

Their actions and choices, also part of the debate.

For fate is not just about our own will

But also about the actions and choices of others still

For the web of fate, is a complex one

And we are all connected, like the rays of the sun.

And as we navigate this web of fate,

We must remember, that we are not just our own fate

For the fate of others, is also in our hands

And we must strive to make a difference, in this grand plan.

For our actions and choices, can shape not just our own fate

But also the fate of others, in this grand debate

So let us not be slaves to fate's whims

But rather, let us take control of our own limbs

For in the grand scheme of things, fate doth play

A role in our lives, but it is not the only way

For our fate is not just predetermined,

But also created by the choices we make and the paths we've chosen.

We must remember that fate is not a straight line

But a winding path, that is not always benign

For fate may lead us to unexpected places

And through the darkest of times and spaces.

But in these moments, we must not falter

For fate is not the end, but the beginning of a new chapter

For fate may bring us to the edge of despair

But it is in these moments, that we learn to care

For ourselves and others, and to strive for the best

For fate may be the test, but it is not the final rest

For in the grand scheme of things, fate doth play

A role in our lives, but it is not the only way

So let us not be slaves to fate's whims

But rather, let us take control of our own limbs

For our fate is not just predetermined,

But also created by the choices we make, and the paths we've chosen.

For fate may be a part of our lives,

But it is not the end, nor is it the prize

For our fate is not just about where we end up

But the journey, that is the true cup.

But let us not forget, that fate is not just about our own lives

But also about the fate of others and the world at large.

For fate is not just about our own personal gain

But also about the impact we have on others and the pain

That we may cause, if we do not tread with care

For our actions and choices, can shape the fate of those who share

This world with us, and we must strive to make a difference,

For the fate of others, is also in our hands, and it's a balance

That we must keep, as we navigate this grand scheme

For fate is not just about our own fate, but also the fate of the team

So let us not be slaves to fate's whims

But rather, let us take control of our own limbs

For in the grand scheme of things, fate doth play

A role in our lives, but it is not the only way

For our fate is not just predetermined,

But also created by the choices we make and the paths we've chosen

And as we journey through this grand scheme,

We must remember, that our fate is not just about our own dream

But also about the fate of others and the world,

And we must strive to make a difference, and not be unfurled

By the winds of fate, but rather, take control

For it is in our hands, that our fate unfolds.

And as we journey through this grand scheme,

We must remember that fate is not always what it seems

For it is not just about the paths that we take

But also about the way we navigate through life's twists and breaks

For fate is not just about the end result

But also about the journey, and how we felt

For fate may bring us to unexpected places

But it is in these moments that we learn to embrace

The unknown, and find the strength within

For fate may lead us to the edge of the abyss, but it's not the end

For fate is not just about the destination

But also about the way we learn to adapt, and find our own sensation

So let us not be slaves to fate's whims

But rather, let us take control of our own limbs

For in the grand scheme of things, fate doth play

A role in our lives, but it is not the only way

For our fate is not just predetermined

But also created by the choices we make, and the paths we've chosen

And as we journey through this grand scheme,

We must remember, that our fate is not just about our own dream

But also about the fate of others and the world,

And we must strive to make a difference, and not be unfurled

By the winds of fate, but rather, take control

For it is in our hands, that our fate unfolds. And that's the goal.

9. Realm of Beauty, Heart of Art

In the realm of beauty and form,
Where creativity and skill are born,
There lies a realm of art, so grand,
That it doth transcend and understand
The very essence of our being,
The depths of thought and endless seeing,
For art is not just brush and paint,
But the very soul that doth acquaint
The world with beauty, truth, and light,
It is the mirror that doth ignite
The fire of imagination,
The wellspring of inspiration
But art is not just for the few,
It is for all, both me and you,
For it is the voice of humanity,
The symphony of diversity
It doth challenge and provoke,
It doth make us laugh, it doth make us choke,
It doth make us feel, it doth make us think,
It is the very essence of what it means to be human and to link
Our hearts and minds to something greater,
To a realm beyond the worldly chatter,
For art is not just something to see,
But a journey of self-discovery.
So let us embrace the beauty of art,
For it is the beating heart
Of our very existence,

And in it, true transcendence.
And though art may take many forms,
From poetry to sculpture, music to storms,
It is not just the product that matters,
But the process that doth scatter
The seeds of creativity and growth,
For in art, we find our own worth.
It is the reflection of our souls,
The culmination of our goals,
For art is not just something to behold,
But a means to express and to mold
Our innermost thoughts and desires,
To reach for the stars, to climb higher.
But art is not just for the artist,
It is for all, to be cherished,
For it doth bring us together,
To share in the beauty, to treasure
The moments of joy and of pain,
To feel alive and to remain
Connected to something greater than ourselves,
For art is not just a thing, but an experience that delves
Into the depths of the human spirit,
To find meaning, to find merit.
So let us embrace the power of art,
For it is the key to the human heart,
And in it, we shall find our way,
To a brighter tomorrow, to a brighter day.
But art is not just a means to an end,
It is the very fabric that doth extend
Beyond the boundaries of time and space,
It is the legacy we leave in its place.

For art is not just a fleeting thing,
But a timeless treasure that doth bring
Joy and inspiration for generations,
A source of wonder and admiration.
It is the reflection of our culture,
The embodiment of our future.
But art is not just for the elite,
It is for all, to make complete
Our understanding of the world,
To break down barriers, to unfurl
The potential of the human mind,
To push the boundaries and to bind
Us together in a common goal,
To make the world a better whole.
So let us embrace the beauty of art,
For it is the light that doth start
A fire in our hearts and souls,
And in it, we shall find our role.
For art is not just a thing to see,
But a journey of self-discovery.
But with art, also comes critique,
For not all that is created, is unique.
For art is not just about pleasing,
But about challenging and releasing
The emotions that lie within,
To question the status quo and to spin
A new perspective on reality,
To push boundaries and to free
The mind from the shackles of the mundane,
To find beauty in the profane.
And though art may be divisive,

It is through diversity, that it thrives.
For art is not just a solitary pursuit,
But a collective endeavor that doth refute
The notion of one right way,
To open our eyes to the beauty of diversity each day.
So let us embrace the complexities of art,
For it is through its contradictions, that we start
To understand the human condition,
And in it, find our own mission.
And so, as we journey through this realm of art,
We must remember to keep an open heart.
For art is not just about what we see,
But about the emotions it evokes in thee.
It is not just about the final result,
But about the process, the journey, the jolt.
For art is not just about perfection,
But about expression and self-reflection.
It is not just about the artist's fame,
But about the impact it has on the game.
For art is not just about the form,
But about the message, the story, the norm.
So let us not be swayed by the critics,
For art is not just about politics.
Let us embrace the beauty of art,
For it is the mirror that doth impart
The truest reflection of who we are,
And in it, we shall find the stars.
For art is not just a thing to behold,
But a means to transcend and to be bold.
So let us embrace the power of art,
For it is the key to the human heart.

But let us not forget,

That art also has its debt.

For in the creation of art,

There is a tearing apart

Of the natural world around us,

And the impact it doth thus.

For art is not just about expression,

But also about compassion and discretion.

We must consider the cost,

Of the materials and resources lost.

And in our pursuit of beauty and form,

We must strive for sustainability, the norm.

For art is not just about the self,

But about the health and well-being of all else.

So let us not only create,

But also consider and regulate.

For in the creation of art,

We have a responsibility to play our part

In preserving and protecting,

The world and all its intersecting.

So let us embrace the beauty of art,

But also be mindful of its heart.

And as we continue to explore the realm of art,

Let us remember that it is not just a matter of heart.

Art is not just about feelings and emotions,

But also about intellect and notions.

For art is not just a matter of taste,

But a reflection of the human race.

It is a window into our history,

And a glimpse of our destiny.

It is not just a thing to be admired,

But a tool to be studied and inquired.
For art is not just entertainment,
But a means of education.
It teaches us about culture and society,
And helps us to see the world more clearly.
So let us not just appreciate art,
But also critically engage and depart
With a deeper understanding and wisdom,
For art is not just a form of freedom,
But also a form of responsibility,
To use it for the betterment of humanity.
And as we delve deeper into the realm of art,
Let us remember that it is not just a work of heart.
For art is not just a matter of personal expression,
But also a means of collective expression.
It is not just about the individual artist,
But about the community and its persistence.
For art is not just a solitary pursuit,
But a collective endeavor that doth refute
The notion of isolation and division,
And embraces the power of collaboration and fusion.
Art is not just a medium for self-expression,
But also a means of social and cultural expression.
It is not just about personal gain,
But about the greater good and the common refrain.
So let us not just create for ourselves,
But also for the betterment of our communities and shelves.
For art is not just about the individual,
But about the collective, the community, and its survival.
So let us embrace the beauty of art,
But also its power to bring us together and play our part.

And as we continue to explore the realm of art,
Let us remember that it is not just a matter of heart.
For art is not just a fleeting thing,
But a timeless treasure that doth bring
Joy and inspiration for generations,
A source of wonder and admiration.
But art is not just something to be admired,
It is something to be experienced and desired.
For art is not just something to see,
But something to feel and to be.
It is not just something to look at,
But something to engage with and interact.
For art is not just a passive experience,
But an active one that doth enhance
Our understanding and connection,
To the world and to one's own reflection.
So let us not just admire art,
But also actively engage and depart
With a deeper understanding and connection,
For art is not just a form of expression,
But also a form of engagement and immersion.
And as we continue to delve into the realm of art,
Let us remember that it is not just a matter of heart.
For art is not just a means of self-expression,
But also a means of self-reflection.
It is not just about the external,
But also about the internal.
For art is not just a way to express,
But also a way to process.
It is not just about putting our thoughts on display,
But also about working through them in a way.

Art is not just about showing the world who we are,

But also about understanding ourselves and what we are.

It is not just about the final product,

But also about the journey and the impact.

So let us not just create for others to see,

But also for ourselves, to be set free.

For art is not just about external validation,

But also about internal liberation.

So let us embrace the beauty of art,

But also its power to heal the heart.

And as we continue to explore the realm of art,

Let us remember that it is not just a matter of heart.

For art is not just a means of self-expression,

But also a means of communication.

It is not just about putting our thoughts on display,

But also about connecting and conveying

Ideas, emotions, and stories to others,

And fostering understanding and empathy towards brothers.

Art is not just about self-expression,

But about the expression of humanity and its obsession

With making sense of the world and our place in it,

Through the medium of imagination and wit.

So let us not just create for ourselves,

But also for the betterment of our relationship with others and shelves.

For art is not just about personal gain,

But about the power of connection and communication to sustain

The human experience and our sense of community,

So let us embrace the beauty of art, and its ability to foster unity.

And as we continue to delve into the realm of art,

Let us remember that it is not just a matter of heart.

For art is not just a product of the present,

But also a reflection of the past and a hint of the future's ascent.
It is not just about the here and now,
But also about the history and how
It has shaped and influenced our society,
And how it will shape our future's destiny.
Art is not just about the individual artist's vision,
But also about the collective tradition and decision
Of a culture and its evolution,
Through the ages and its resolution.
So let us not just appreciate art for its aesthetic value,
But also for its historical and cultural relevance.
For art is not just a form of entertainment,
But also a form of education and enlightenment.
So let us embrace the beauty of art,
But also its power to educate and impart
A deeper understanding of our past,
And a glimpse into our future at last.
And as we continue to explore the realm of art,
Let us remember that it is not just a matter of heart.
For art is not just a product of the human mind,
But also a product of the human condition.
It is not just about the creative process,
But also about the struggles and the stress.
For art is not just about beauty and grace,
But also about the dark and the pain.
It is not just about the light and the good,
But also about the shadows and the misunderstood.
Art is not just about the surface level,
But also about the depths and the devil.
So let us not just appreciate art for its aesthetic value,
But also for its emotional and psychological significance.

For art is not just a form of expression,

But also a form of catharsis and suppression.

So let us embrace the beauty of art,

But also its power to heal and to impart

A deeper understanding of the human condition,

And the complexities that lie within.

And as we delve deeper into the realm of art,

Let us remember that it is not just a matter of heart.

For art is not just a product of human creativity,

But also a product of human diversity.

It is not just about one culture or one perspective,

But about the melting pot of perspectives.

For art is not just about a singular style,

But about the fusion and the variation of the pile.

It is not just about one form of expression,

But about the spectrum of expression.

Art is not just about one type of beauty,

But about the diversity and the plurality.

So let us not just appreciate art for its aesthetic value,

But also for its diversity and its ability

to showcase the different perspectives,

and the beauty in the contrasts.

For art is not just a form of expression,

But also a form of representation and inclusion.

So let us embrace the beauty of art,

But also its power to unite and depart

With a deeper understanding and appreciation,

Of the diverse human experience and its liberation.

10. The Paradox of Time: A Journey through Cosmic Sands

Time, a force both grand and fleeting,

A concept that's both complex and fleeting,

A puzzle that's yet to be completed,

A mystery that's yet to be defeated.

In physics, it's a dimension,

In philosophy, a conundrum,

In our lives, it's a measure,

In our hearts, it's a treasure.

Einstein's theory of relativity,

Shook our understanding of time's velocity,

It's not constant, but relative,

A concept that's hard to conceive.

But what is time, truly,

Is it a mere human construct,

Or something that's truly

A fundamental aspect?

Time, it moves forward, never backward,

A one-way street, a never-ending march,

It erodes all, it destroys all,

Yet it gives life, it creates all.

Time, it's a reminder of our mortality,

A constant countdown to our finality,

But it's also a teacher, a guide,

Showing us the value of living with pride.

In the end, time is a paradox,

A puzzle with no clear box,

But one thing is clear,
Time is something we hold dear.
So let us make the most of it,
Let us not waste a single bit,
For time is precious and fleeting,
A force that's both grand and fleeting.
But as we journey through this timeline,
We must remember, it's not just a climb,
It's not just a race to the end,
But a journey, with twists and bends.
The past, the present, and the future,
All intertwined, a cosmic suture,
The memories we've made,
Are etched in our hearts, never to fade.
The present, a fleeting moment,
A chance to live, to love, to augment,
The future, a mystery, yet to unfold,
A canvas, ready to be painted, with stories untold.
Time, it's a force that's both destructive and constructive,
A reminder of our mortality, yet an opportunity to be productive,
It's a teacher that shows us the value of life,
And the importance of living with purpose, and not just strife.
So let us cherish every moment,
And make the most of it, with every component,
For time is a gift, not to be squandered,
But to be used wisely, and never squandered.
In the end, time will be our judge,
A record of our lives, and our grudge,
But let us not fear, for we have the power,
To shape our own destiny, in this cosmic hour.
For time is not just a force,

But a tool, to be wielded with care,
A reminder of our mortality, yet a chance to be aware,
And to live our lives, with meaning and grace, in this cosmic space.
And as we journey through this cosmic expanse,
We must remember, time is but a chance,
A chance to grow, to learn, to evolve,
To find our place, in this grand resolve.
For time, is not just a measure of our days,
But a reflection of our deeds, and our ways,
It's the legacy we leave behind,
And the memories we make, that bind.
And as we stand at the edge of time,
We must remember, it's not just a climb,
It's not just a race to the end,
But a journey, with twists and bends.
For time is not just a force that destroys,
But a force that creates, and employs,
A force that shapes, and molds,
And makes us who we are, bold.
So let us embrace the passage of time,
And make the most of it, with every chime,
For time is a gift, not to be wasted,
But to be cherished, and embraced.
For time is not just a force,
But a companion, to be with us, always, of course,
A reminder of our mortality, yet a chance to be alive,
And to make the most of our time, as we strive.
And as we journey through the sands of time,
Let us not forget, it's not just a climb,
It's not just a race to the end,
But a journey, with purpose and bend.

For time is not just a measure of our days,

But a reflection of our choices, and our ways,

It's the story of our lives, and our fate,

And the impact we make, that won't abate.

So let us make the most of our time,

Let us not waste a single rhyme,

Let us live with purpose, and with grace,

And leave our mark, in this cosmic race.

For time is not just a force that's fleeting,

But a force that's powerful, and defeating,

A force that shapes, and molds,

And makes us who we are, bold.

So let us embrace the passage of time,

And make the most of it, with every chime,

For time is a gift, not to be wasted,

But to be cherished, and embraced.

And as we journey through the realms of time,

Let us not forget, it's not just a climb,

It's not just a race to the end,

But a journey, with meaning and bend.

For time is not just a measure of our days,

But a reflection of our actions, and our ways,

It's the story of our lives, and our fate,

And the memories we create, that won't abate.

So let us make the most of our time,

Let us not waste a single rhyme,

Let us live with intention, and with heart,

And leave our mark, before we depart.

For time is not just a force that's fleeting,

But a force that's powerful, and defeating,

A force that shapes, and molds,

And makes us who we are, bold.
So let us embrace the passage of time,
And make the most of it, with every chime,
For time is a gift, not to be squandered,
But to be cherished, and pondered.
For time, is the very essence of our existence,
And the very purpose of our persistence,
And as we journey through this cosmic expanse,
Let us make the most of our time, and our chance.
But as we journey through the ages of time,
Let us not forget, that it's not just a climb,
It's not just a race to the end,
But a journey, with purpose and a friend.
For time is not just a measure of our days,
But a reflection of our journey, and our ways,
It's the story of our lives, and our fate,
And the legacy we create, that won't abate.
So let us make the most of our time,
Let us not waste a single rhyme,
Let us live with compassion, and with love,
And leave our mark, in the stars above.
For time is not just a force that's fleeting,
But a force that's powerful, and defeating,
A force that shapes, and molds,
And makes us who we are, bold.
So let us embrace the passage of time,
And make the most of it, with every chime,
For time is a gift, not to be taken lightly,
But to be cherished, and used rightly.
For time, is the very essence of our being,
And the very purpose of our seeing,

And as we journey through this cosmic expanse,
Let us make the most of our time, and our chance.
Let us make our mark, in the annals of time,
And let our legacy, forever shine,
For time is not just a force, but a friend,
Guiding us through to the very end.

11. The Gender Journey: Navigating Complexities, Celebrating Diversity, and Building Inclusion

'Twas in the realm of science and philosophy

That the topic of gender did often arise,

With discussions deep and musings quite lofty,

On the nature of self and the gender guise.

Some argued that gender is but a social construct,

A label imposed by society's hand,

And that true self is found in the individual,

Free from the constraints of gender's band.

Others believed that gender is innate,

A product of biology and genes,

That the sexes are distinct and separate,

And that our gender identity prefigures.

But what of those who fall outside the binary,

Who do not fit into "man" or "woman" neat,

Are they to be denied their identity,

Or relegated to a marginalized seat?

And so we delve into the complexities,

Of gender, self, and societal norms,

For though we may not have all the answers,

It is through discourse that wisdom is born.

Thus, let us continue to ponder and question,

The nature of gender and its role,

For in understanding, acceptance and inclusion,

We can break free from the gender parole.

But as we delve deeper, we must also consider,

The impact of gender on society,

For though individuals have agency,

Structural inequalities still hold sway.

Men and women are not equal in outcome,

Due to systemic bias and discrimination,

And though we strive for gender equality,

We must acknowledge and address this alienation.

Furthermore, the gender spectrum is vast,

And each person's experience unique,

We must listen to and amplify,

The voices of those who are marginalized and seek.

For only through empathy and understanding,

Can we truly create a society,

Where all genders are accepted and respected,

And individuals can authentically be.

So let us continue on this journey,

Of exploration and self-discovery,

For in unraveling the mysteries of gender,

We can create a more just and equitable society.

But as we progress, let us not forget,

The intersectionality of identity,

For gender is but one aspect,

Of the self and one's reality.

Race, class, sexuality, ability,

All shape one's experiences and struggles,

And to truly create an inclusive society,

We must consider all these factors and juggles.

And so we are tasked with a great undertaking,

To unravel the complexities of gender and self,

To create a society where all are free to be,

And all identities are recognized and felt.

It is a long and winding path we tread,

But one worth taking for the sake of all,

For in embracing the diversity of gender,

We can build a society that is just and tall.

So let us continue to question, ponder and debate,

As we strive towards understanding and acceptance,

For only in embracing the complexities,

Can we create a truly inclusive and transcendent.

And as we journey on, let us not forget,

The impact of gender on the natural world,

For the balance and harmony of nature,

Is also affected by the societal swirl.

The effects of climate change and pollution,

Are felt disproportionately by women,

And the toxic masculinity culture,

Leads to the exploitation of the earth and glen.

Thus, we must recognize the interconnectedness,

Of gender, society and the environment,

And work towards a sustainable future,

Where all can thrive and be content.

But it is not only about actions and policy,

But also the way we think and perceive,

For a shift in consciousness and perspective,

Is also necessary to truly believe.

And so we must continue to educate ourselves,

And strive towards a more equitable and sustainable world,

For only in embracing the complexities of gender,

Can we create a harmonious and peaceful swirl.

As we progress on this journey,

We must also acknowledge,

That gender norms and expectations,

Vary across cultures and backgrounds.

What is considered "masculine" or "feminine"

In one society, may not hold true in another,

And to truly create an inclusive society,

We must celebrate and respect cultural diversity and cover.

But we must also be aware,

Of the ways in which colonialism,

Has imposed Western gender norms,

On cultures and societies, leading to a malign.

And so, decolonization and cultural preservation,

Is also crucial in this discourse,

For only in understanding and respecting,

Different cultural perspectives, can we truly endorse.

And so, let us continue to learn and grow,

As we navigate the complexities of gender,

For only in embracing diversity and understanding,

Can we create a truly inclusive and equitable splendor.

And as we move forward, let us not forget,

The importance of representation and visibility,

For the media and society,

often present a limited and limiting reality.

The lack of representation and visibility,

of marginalized genders, leads to invisibility and erasure,

And reinforces societal biases and inequalities,

Making it harder for marginalized individuals to find a secure.

Thus, it is crucial that we actively work towards,

Increasing representation and visibility,

For only in seeing ourselves reflected,

Can we truly believe in our own possibility.

It is also important to recognize,

The power of language and words,

For the way we talk about gender,

can reinforce or challenge societal norms and herds.

And so, let us continue to educate ourselves,

On the power of language and representation,

For only in using inclusive language and amplifying diverse voices,

Can we create a truly equitable and just foundation.

As we delve deeper into the complexities of gender,

It is important to remember that it is a fluid and ever-changing construct.

Individuals have the right to define and express their own gender identity,

and it is not for others to question or restrict.

Gender expression and gender identity are distinct,

and one's expression may not align with societal expectations or stereotypes.

It is important to respect and support individuals in their self-expression and identity,

and to create a society where all forms of gender expression are accepted and respected.

Additionally, the concept of non-binary and gender non-conforming individuals,

highlights the limitations of the traditional binary understanding of gender.

It is important to recognize and respect the diversity within the gender spectrum and to create a society that is inclusive of all identities.

Furthermore, the concept of gender identity

and expression is not limited to human beings,

and it is important to also consider the diversity

of gender within the animal kingdom and in nature.

But as we strive towards an inclusive society,

Let us not forget the importance of self-exploration,

For everyone's gender journey is unique,

And one's relationship with gender is a personal sensation.

It is important to give oneself the space,

To question and explore one's own gender identity,

Without fear of judgement or societal pressure,

For only then can one's true self be free.

It is also important to recognize,

That one's relationship with gender,

Can change and evolve over time,

And that it is okay to not have a clear line.

And so, let us continue to support,

Each other's individual journeys,

For only in embracing the complexities,

Can we create a society where all genders are honored and cherished.

As we ponder on the topic of gender,

Let us remember that it is a complex and nuanced one,

But through understanding, acceptance and empathy,

We can create a society where all genders are celebrated and none are undone.

But as we move forward, we must also acknowledge

the ways in which gender impacts one's mental and physical health,

For societal pressures and expectations,

can lead to negative consequences and stealth.

The gender binary and societal expectations,

can lead to body image issues and disordered eating,

and toxic masculinity culture,

can lead to a lack of emotional expression, and a relationship unhealing.

It is important to recognize and address,

the ways in which societal norms and expectations,

can contribute to mental and physical health issues,

and work towards creating a society where individuals can be their authentic

selves, without fear of being dismissed.

And so, let us continue to educate ourselves,

on the ways in which gender impacts one's well-being,

and work towards creating a society where individuals can thrive,

and all genders are respected, accepted, and free from suffering.

As we delve into the complexities of gender,

let us remember that it is a multifaceted and ever-evolving topic,

But through understanding, acceptance, and empathy,

we can create a society where all genders are celebrated and respected, and humanity can flourish and prosper.

But as we continue on this journey, let us not forget,

the ways in which gender also intersects with other identities,

such as race, class, ability, and sexuality,

and how these intersections shape one's experiences and realities.

For individuals from marginalized communities,

the struggles and challenges they face,

are often compounded by societal biases and discrimination,

based on their intersectional identities and place.

It is important to recognize and acknowledge,

these intersections and how they contribute,

to the systemic inequalities that exist,

and work towards creating a more equitable and inclusive society that is astute.

And so, let us continue to educate ourselves,

on the ways in which different identities intersect,

and work towards creating a society,

where all individuals are treated with dignity and respect,

regardless of their gender, race, class, ability, or sexual orientation,

and where intersectional equality is the norm, and not an exception.

As we ponder on the complexities of gender,

let us remember that it is a multifaceted and ever-evolving topic,

But through understanding, acceptance, and empathy,

we can create a society where all genders are celebrated,

respected and where intersectional equality is the norm,

and humanity can thrive and prosper in harmony.

But as we move forward, let us not forget,

the ways in which gender impacts and is impacted by,

the economy and the workplace.

Gender pay gap, lack of representation in leadership positions,

and gender discrimination in the workplace,

are just some of the ways in which gender affects one's economic status and fate.

It is important to recognize and address these issues,

and work towards creating a more equitable and inclusive economy,

where individuals are paid and treated fairly,

regardless of their gender and ability.

And so, let us continue to educate ourselves,

on the ways in which gender affects the economy and the workplace,

and work towards creating a society where individuals can thrive,

and all genders are respected, accepted, and have equal opportunities to succeed

and make their own way.

As we delve into the complexities of gender,

let us remember that it is a multifaceted and ever-evolving topic,

But through understanding, acceptance, and empathy,

we can create a society where all genders are celebrated, respected,

and have equal opportunities to succeed, in all aspects of life.

But as we continue on this journey, let us not forget,

the ways in which gender affects and is affected by,

the education system and the knowledge we acquire.

Gender bias in education, lack of representation of marginalized genders in curriculum,

and gender discrimination in academic settings,

are just some of the ways in which gender affects one's educational journey and fire.

It is important to recognize and address these issues,

and work towards creating a more equitable and inclusive education system,

where individuals are treated fairly,

regardless of their gender and ability, and have access to the knowledge they desire.

And so, let us continue to educate ourselves,

on the ways in which gender affects the education system,

and work towards creating a society where individuals can thrive,

and all genders are respected, accepted, and have equal opportunities to learn and acquire knowledge.

As we delve into the complexities of gender,

let us remember that it is a multifaceted and ever-evolving topic,

But through understanding, acceptance, and empathy,

we can create a society where all genders are celebrated, respected,

and have equal opportunities to learn and acquire knowledge, in all aspects of life.

But as we move forward, let us not forget,

the ways in which gender affects and is affected by,

the healthcare system and the care we receive.

It is important to recognize and address these issues,

and work towards creating a more equitable and inclusive healthcare system,

where individuals are treated fairly,

regardless of their gender and ability, and have access to the care they need.

And so, let us continue to educate ourselves,

on the ways in which gender affects the healthcare system,

and work towards creating a society where individuals can thrive,

and all genders are respected, accepted, and have equal access to quality healthcare.

As we delve into the complexities of gender,

let us remember that it is a multifaceted and ever-evolving topic,

But through understanding, acceptance, and empathy,

we can create a society where all genders are celebrated, respected, and have equal access to quality healthcare in all aspects of life.

12. The Mystery of Sex: Embracing the Complexities

In copulation, there lies a mystery

A joining of two forms, in love's sweet history

A dance of bodies, with purpose and intent

As hormones and pheromones, their signals are sent

But what of the science, that underlies this act

The genetic code, that makes us all react

The chromosomes, that dictate who we'll be

The X and Y, that set our destiny

And what of the philosophy, that shapes our desire

The longing for connection, that sets our hearts on fire

The search for completeness, that fuels our pursuit

The yearning for unity, that makes our souls compute

But there is also a dark side, to this carnal dance

The objectification, the manipulation, the chance

That love and pleasure, will be twisted and bent

And used for power, in a way that's not meant

So let us remember, as we engage in this rite

The beauty and wonder, but also the fight

To always see the other, as a subject, not an object

And to honor consent, in all that we subject.

But there is also the question of identity,

Of how we define ourselves, in terms of sexuality.

Do we conform to societal norms,

Or do we forge our own paths, in defiance of the storms?

What is the role of gender, in this intimate scene?

Is it a social construct, or a biological supreme?

And what of those who do not fit the binary mold,
Are they any less worthy, of love to behold?
Such questions are not easily answered,
For they delve deep into the psyche, and the soul,
But what is certain, is that sex is not a one-dimensional goal,
But a complex tapestry, of biology, psychology, and social.
As we continue to evolve, as a species and as individuals,
Let us strive to understand, and to accept, the diversity that sex perpetuates.
Let us not be constrained by dogma or prejudice,
But instead, let us embrace, the beauty and wonder, that sex produces.
So let us honor the mystery, of this sacred act,
And let us approach it, with respect, and with tact.
For in the end, it is not just about the physical,
But about the connection, that we make, that is truly spiritual.
And what of the future, what does it hold
For the way we view sex, and the stories it tells?
Will we continue to evolve, in our understanding,
Or will we remain stagnant, in our demanding?
Will technology change the way we interact,
In matters of love and sex, and the contracts we make?
Will AI and robots, be part of the equation,
And will they be able to mimic the sensation?
Will we overcome the taboo and the shame,
That surrounds sex and pleasure, and give it a name?
Will we break the barriers, and change the narrative,
To make sex a positive force, for all to experience.
These are questions, that only time will tell,
But as we ponder and ponder, one thing is well,
That sex is a fundamental part, of the human experience,
And it will continue to shape, our existence.
So let us continue to explore, the depths of sex,

And let us break the bounds, of what we expect.

For in doing so, we may just find,

That sex is not just a physical act, but a state of mind.

So let us strive to understand sex,

in all its complexities and nuances,

let us not be afraid to ask questions,

and seek answers to the unknowns.

Let us not let society's expectations,

shape our perceptions of sex,

let us not let fear and shame,

hold us back from experiencing it.

Let us not let the past,

define our views on sex,

let us look to the future,

with an open and curious mind.

For in understanding sex,

we understand ourselves,

our desires, our needs,

our very humanity.

So let us embrace sex,

not as a taboo, but as a natural part of life,

let us break the barriers,

and let our true selves shine.

For in doing so,

we open ourselves to new possibilities,

to new connections,

to new forms of love and intimacy.

So let us not shy away from the topic of sex,

but instead, let us embrace it,

with open arms, and open hearts.

For in the end, the mystery and wonder of sex is what makes life worth living.

But let us not forget, the importance of safety,

In all our sexual interactions, be they casual or intimate.

Consent must always be given, and boundaries respected,

For true pleasure and connection, can only be achieved, when all parties are invested.

Let us educate ourselves, on the risks and prevention,

Of sexually transmitted infections and unwanted pregnancies.

And let us also educate ourselves, on the emotional and psychological,

Aspects of sex, to ensure healthy relationships and satisfaction.

For sex is not just a physical act, but an emotional and mental one as well.

It is a means of connection, not just between bodies, but between souls as well.

So let us approach sex, with care and consideration,

For ourselves and for our partners, in all its manifestations.

For in doing so, we can truly experience,

The beauty, wonder and mystery, that sex has to offer, in all its glory.

Sex is a complex and multi-faceted topic,

That touches upon science, philosophy, and the human experience.

Let us approach it with openness, curiosity, and respect,

As we continue to unravel its mysteries and wonders, with every passing day.

And in the end, let us remember,

That sex is not just a physical act, but a spiritual one as well.

It is a means of connection, not just between bodies, but between souls as well.

It is a way to explore and express, our deepest desires and needs,

And to find a sense of completeness, in the embrace of another.

Sex is not just a means of procreation,

But a way to experience pleasure, and to find connection.

It is a way to explore ourselves, and to understand others,

And to find a sense of belonging, in the world around us.

So let us not shy away from the topic of sex,

But instead, let us embrace it, with open arms, and open hearts.

For in the end, the beauty and wonder of sex, is what makes life worth living.

It is an intimate, a profound and a sacred act,

That can bring us closer to ourselves and to others,

It is a way to explore our deepest selves,

And to find meaning in the world around us.

So let us approach sex with care, and with respect,

And let us always strive to understand,

It's complexities and nuances,

As we continue to unravel its mysteries, with every passing day.

And let us not forget, that sex is also a political act,

A means of asserting power, and of challenging oppression.

It is a way to claim agency, and to fight for equality,

And to demand respect, for all bodies, regardless of gender, sexual orientation,

or ability.

Sexuality is a fundamental aspect of who we are,

It shapes our identity, and our sense of self.

It is a means of expressing our individuality,

And of connecting with others, on a deeply personal level.

So let us continue to push the boundaries,

Of what is considered acceptable and taboo,

Let us continue to challenge the status quo,

And strive for a world where sex is celebrated, rather than stigmatized.

In conclusion, sex is a complex and multifaceted topic,

That touches upon science, philosophy, and the human experience.

Let us approach it with openness, curiosity, and respect,

As we continue to unravel its mysteries and wonders, with every passing day.

It is a way to connect with ourselves and others,

To find pleasure, intimacy, and meaning in our lives.

Let us celebrate it, and let us continue to explore it,

As we journey through this wonderful and mysterious thing we call life.

13. Quest for Verity: Uncovering the Mysteries of the Meek, Truth Within and Beyond

Verity, the elusive muse of those who seek
To unravel the mysteries of the meek
And pierce the veil of falsehood and deceit
With reason as their guide, and logic as their fleet
But what is truth, and wherefore doth it dwell?
Is it a thing that can be known, or is it just a spell?
A mirage that dances on the desert sand
A will-o'-the-wisp that leads one to a barren land
Perchance it is a thing that's writ within
The very fabric of the soul and spirit,
A guiding light that shines upon the path
That leads to wisdom, and to knowledge's aftermath
Or mayhap truth is but a fleeting breeze
That whispers through the trees
A symphony that plays upon the ear
A symphony that's always just out of reach
Yet still, we strive to catch a glimpse of it
To bask in its ethereal light and know it
For truth is the eternal quest we undertake
And the reward for which we'll gladly sacrifice our fate
Thus, let us seek the truth with valor and with might
For in the search for truth, there is no end in sight.
But in our quest for truth, we must be wary
For the path is fraught with perils, dark and hairy

For oftentimes, the truth is shrouded in disguise
And those who seek it, are met with bitter lies
The mind is but a fragile thing, prone to decay
And in its frailty, it can easily stray
From the path of righteousness, and fall to vice
And in the end, be led to sacrifice
The truth for falsehood, and the light for dark
And in so doing, lose the very spark
That guides us on our journey, and sets us free
From the shackles of ignorance, and the bonds of misery
So let us tread with care, and with an open mind
For the truth is not always easy to find
And though we may stumble, and falter in our quest
We must persevere, and put our doubts to rest
For in the end, it is the truth that sets us free
And gives our souls the wings to soar and be
And in the quest for truth, we find our way
To a brighter tomorrow, and a better day.
But alas, the truth is not for all to see
For some choose to live in their own reality
Closed off to the world, and the truth it holds
A prison of their own making, their minds and hearts caged and cold
And so, we must not only seek the truth for ourselves
But also strive to open the eyes of those on the shelf
For the truth is not meant to be kept hidden away
But shared and spread, for the betterment of each and every day
And as we journey forth, in search of the truth
Let us not forget, that it takes but a single youth
To change the world, with a single shining light
And bring forth the truth, with all its might
So let us be the ones who guide the way

And show the world the truth, come what may
For in the end, it is the truth that shall prevail
And bring forth a new dawn, a new story to tell.
But even as we strive to bring forth the truth,
We must also remember that it can be a bitter fruit
For sometimes the truth can be a heavy load
And the weight of it can leave us feeling cold
It can tear apart the fabric of our lives
And leave us questioning all that we believe
It can shatter our illusions and our dreams
And leave us feeling empty, or like a broken ream
But even so, we must not shy away
From the truth, come what may
For it is only through facing it head on
That we can truly learn to move on
So let us be courageous and true
In our quest for the truth, and what it can do
For though it may be hard and it may be tough
It is the only way to rise above
For in the end, it is the truth that shall lead us to the light
And bring us to a new dawn, with a new day in sight.
But there is one truth that is often overlooked
It is the truth that lies within the heart and the nook
It is the truth of one's own self and the quest for self-discovery
It is the truth that leads to inner peace, love, and mastery.
One must take the time to look within
To question the self, and to peel the skin
Off the layers of illusion, and face the core
For it is only then, that one can truly soar
The journey to self-truth may be long and winding
But it is a journey worth taking, always binding

For in the end, it is the truth of the self

That brings true happiness, love, and wealth.

Thus, let us strive to seek the truth in all its forms

To look within and without, to weather all the storms

For it is the truth that shall set us free

And bring forth a new dawn, a new destiny.

But as we seek the truth, we must also be mindful

Of the impact it may have, both positive and unkind

For the truth, though freeing, can also bring pain

And leave deep scars, that may never fully regain

Therefore, we must handle the truth with care

And be cognizant of the burden it may bear

We must be considerate of others and their plight

And use the truth as a tool for healing and right

For the truth, though powerful, can also be divisive

It can be used to hurt, and to be manipulative

Thus, we must strive to use the truth with integrity

And always strive to promote empathy

For the truth, is not just a thing to be sought

But also a thing to be taught

We must be vigilant in spreading the truth,

Not just for ourselves, but for the betterment of all youth.

Thus, let us seek the truth, in all its forms

And use it as a tool for progress, not for storms

For the truth shall bring forth a new day,

A brighter tomorrow, where love and wisdom will stay.

But as we seek the truth, let us not forget

That it is a thing that is ever-changing, not set

For the truth is not a thing that can be confined

It is a thing that is ever-evolving, not confined

It is something that is ever-growing, not static

It is something that is ever-flowing, not erratic

It is something that is ever-expanding, not limited

It is something that is ever-demanding, not timid

Thus, let us be open to new truths and new perspectives

Let us be open to new ways of interpreting and connecting it

Let us be open to new ways of understanding and applying it

For the truth is not a thing to be feared, but embraced and celebrated

Let us be ever-curious, and ever-willing to learn

For the truth is not a thing that can be unlearned

It is a thing that is ever-present, ever-lasting

And it is a thing that is ever-enlightening, ever-casting

Thus, let us seek the truth, with open hearts and open minds

For it is the truth that will guide us to a better life, and a better kind.

But in our quest for truth, let us not forget

That it is a thing that is relative, not absolute

For the truth is not a thing that is the same for all

It is a thing that is perceived differently, by one and all

It is something that is shaped by our experiences and beliefs

It is something that is influenced by our culture and our griefs

It is something that is unique to each individual

And it is something that is constantly evolving, not stable

Thus, let us be open to different truths and different perspectives

Let us be open to different ways of interpreting and connecting it

Let us be open to different ways of understanding and applying it

For the truth is not a thing to be imposed, but understood and respected

Let us be ever-tolerant, and ever-willing to learn

For the truth is not a thing that can be unlearned

It is a thing that is ever-dynamic, ever-shifting

And it is a thing that is ever-enlightening, ever-lifting

Thus, let us seek the truth, with open hearts and open minds

For it is the truth that will guide us to a better life, and a better kind.

But as we seek the truth, let us not forget
That it is a thing that is also subjective, not objective
For the truth is not a thing that is based on facts alone
It is a thing that is also influenced by emotions, bias, and unknown
It is something that is open to interpretation and perception
It is something that can be influenced by one's own cognition
It is something that is open to question and doubt
And it is something that is not always clear, without a route.
Thus, let us be open to the possibility of multiple truths
Let us be open to the idea that truth can change with time and proof
Let us be open to the possibility that our own understanding may be flawed
For the truth is not a thing to be taken for granted, but continually explored
Let us be ever-skeptical, and ever-inquisitive
For the truth is not a thing that can be taken at face value, and be passive
It is a thing that is ever-evolving, ever-challenging
And it is a thing that is ever-enlightening, ever-enriching
Thus, let us seek the truth, with open hearts and open minds
For it is the truth that will guide us to a better life, and a better kind.
But as we seek the truth, let us not forget
That it is a thing that is also personal, not universal
For the truth is not a thing that is the same for all
It is a thing that is different for each and everyone
It is something that is shaped by our own beliefs and values
It is something that is defined by our own experiences and goals
It is something that is unique to each individual's perspective
And it is something that is constantly changing and adapting, not static
Thus, let us be open to the idea that there are multiple truths
Let us be open to the idea that truth can change with time and proof
Let us be open to the possibility that our own understanding may be limited
For the truth is not a thing to be taken for granted, but constantly re-evaluated
Let us be ever-curious, and ever-willing to learn

For the truth is not a thing that can be unlearned

It is a thing that is ever-evolving, ever-dynamic

And it is a thing that is ever-enlightening, ever-enriching

Thus, let us seek the truth, with open hearts and open minds

For it is the truth that will guide us to a better life, and a better kind.

But as we seek the truth, let us not forget

That it is a thing that is also complex, not simple

For the truth is not a thing that can be easily explained

It is a thing that is often shrouded in mystery, and remains

It is something that is multi-faceted and multi-layered

It is something that is often hidden, and not easily uncovered

It is something that is often nuanced and difficult to grasp

And it is something that is often beyond our understanding and clasp.

Thus, let us be open to the idea that the truth is not always straightforward

Let us be open to the idea that truth can be elusive and hard to discern

Let us be open to the possibility that we may never fully understand the truth

For the truth is not a thing to be taken lightly, but constantly sought

Let us be ever-persistent, and ever-diligent

For the truth is not a thing that can be easily found, without effort and commitment

It is a thing that is ever-elusive, ever-complex

And it is a thing that is ever-enlightening, ever-enriching

Thus, let us seek the truth, with open hearts and open minds

For it is the truth that will guide us to a better life, and a better kind.

But as we seek the truth, let us not forget

That it is a thing that is also fluid, not set

For the truth is not a thing that remains the same

It is a thing that changes with time, and with the game

It is something that is adaptable and responsive

It is something that is dynamic and not stagnant

It is something that is ever-evolving, not fixed

And it is something that is always in a state of flux.

Thus, let us be open to the idea that truth is not absolute

Let us be open to the idea that truth can change with time and context

Let us be open to the possibility that our understanding may be incomplete

For the truth is not a thing to be taken for granted, but constantly updated

Let us be ever-flexible, and ever-willing to adjust

For the truth is not a thing that can be set in stone, and be a crust

It is a thing that is ever-changing, ever-evolving

And it is a thing that is ever-enlightening, ever-enriching

Thus, let us seek the truth, with open hearts and open minds

For it is the truth that will guide us to a better life, and a better kind.

14. Veracity: The Intersection of Fact and Emotion

Veracity, a concept oft misunderstood,
A facet of our existence oft befuddled,
For facts, though true, may oft be skewed,
And perceptions oft be muddled.
In science, facts are sine qua non,
A foundation upon which all is built,
But facts alone do not make us omniscient,
For knowledge, too, must be distilled.
Philosophy, too, delves into the fray,
Examining the nature of truth,
For facts, though solid, can lead astray,
If viewed without the lens of proof.
In this world of information overflow,
We must be cautious and discerning,
For facts, though powerful, can be a woe,
If not with wisdom and unlearning.
So let us delve into the depths of fact,
With open minds and critical thought,
For in the pursuit of truth, we must not slack,
And knowledge, to us, shall be brought.
But let us not forget the human touch,
For facts, though cold, can be imbued,
With empathy, understanding, and such,
To better serve the greater good.
For science and philosophy, though distinct,
Are not at odds, but in harmony,

For both seek truth, and both assist,

In shaping our reality.

And as we navigate this complex world,

With facts as our guiding light,

We must not forget the stories unfurled,

That give meaning to our plight.

For facts are not just data to be gleaned,

But pieces of a greater whole,

And it is through the stories we've gleaned,

That our understanding takes its toll.

So let us embrace the facts we find,

And let them shape our understanding,

For in the quest for truth, we are all entwined,

And in it, our destinies are expanding.

But let us not forget the limitations,

Of facts and knowledge, too,

For often, our understanding is based on presumptions,

And not all is as it seems to be true.

It is important to question, to doubt,

To seek multiple perspectives,

For facts, though presented without a bout,

May not be the full spectrum.

And so, as we delve into the realm of fact,

Let us not be complacent,

For to truly understand, we must interact,

With a spirit of constant enhancement.

For facts, though essential, are not the end,

But rather a means to a greater goal,

To understand ourselves and our fellow men,

And to better our world as a whole.

So let us embrace the journey of fact,

With open minds and hearts,
For in the pursuit of truth, there is no set track,
And in it, our enlightenment starts.
But let us not forget the responsibility,
That comes with the pursuit of fact,
For with knowledge comes a duty,
To use it for the greater good, to act.
For facts, though powerful, can be weaponized,
To harm and discriminate,
It is our duty to ensure, they are utilized,
With compassion and empathy to alleviate.
Let us strive for a world, where facts are not just for a select,
But for all to access and understand,
For true knowledge should not be a matter of respect,
But a fundamental right for every man.
Let us embrace the fact,
That truth and knowledge are a journey,
And that it is through constant interaction,
That we can create a better future.
So let us not be afraid of the complexity,
Of facts and the unknown,
For in the pursuit of truth, lies our ability,
To create a better world, our very own.
But let us not forget that facts are not the only truth,
There are also emotions, values, and beliefs,
that shape our perception and give meaning to our youth.
Facts are important, but they are not the whole story,
They are a part of the puzzle, not the key,
To truly understand the human glory,
We must also consider humanity.
In this quest for knowledge, let us not forget,

That facts and emotions are not mutually exclusive,
For it is through the combination, we can truly set
Our hearts and minds free and inclusive.
So let us strive for a balance, in our quest for truth,
A harmony between facts and emotions,
For it is through this balance, that we can truly soothe
And find meaning in our daily commotions.
In the end, let us remember, that facts are important,
But they are not the be-all and end-all,
For to truly understand, we must be present,
In the here and now, and stand tall.
But let us not forget that facts are not always certain,
And that knowledge is ever-evolving,
As new discoveries and perspectives emerge,
Our understanding of the world keeps resolving.
Facts that were once accepted as true,
May be challenged and revised,
It is important to keep an open mind,
And be willing to be surprised.
In this pursuit of knowledge and truth,
Let us not cling to what we know,
For the world is constantly in flux,
And our understanding must also grow.
So let us approach facts with a sense of curiosity,
And a willingness to be wrong,
For it is through this humility,
That we can truly move along.
In the end, let us remember, that facts are a means,
To a deeper understanding of the world,
And that the pursuit of truth, is an ongoing theme,
That keeps our minds and hearts unfurled.

But let us not forget that facts are not the only way,
To understand the world and our place in it,
For there are also other ways, such as art and play,
That can give us a different kind of wit.
Facts can be dry and uninspiring,
But art and play can bring them to life,
They can make the abstract and complex,
Easier to grasp without any strife.
In this quest for knowledge and truth,
Let us not limit ourselves to facts alone,
For there are many other ways to pursue,
A deeper understanding of our own.
So let us approach the world with an open mind,
And a willingness to explore,
For it is through this diversity,
That our understanding can truly soar.
In the end, let us remember, that facts are one way,
To understand the world and our place in it,
But there are many other ways, that can lead us to stay
Engaged and inspired, with a sense of wit.
But let us not forget that facts are not the ultimate goal,
For the pursuit of truth and knowledge is never done,
It is an ongoing journey, that will always roll,
And will keep us searching for the next one.
Facts can be milestones, markers on our path,
But they are not the destination,
For there is always more to discover,
And more to contemplate on.
In this quest for knowledge and truth,
Let us not become complacent,
For there is always more to uncover,

And more to enhance.

So let us approach the world with a sense of wonder,

And a desire to learn and grow,

For it is through this curiosity,

That our understanding will forever flow.

In the end, let us remember, that facts are a step,

In the journey of understanding,

And that the pursuit of truth, is an unending quest,

That will keep us forever expanding.

But let us not forget that facts are not the only thing,

That shape our understanding of the world.

Experience, culture, and upbringing,

All play a role in how we interpret and unfurl.

Facts are objective, but our understanding of them,

Is shaped by our subjective experiences,

It is important to recognize, that facts are not always condemn,

But are open to different interpretations and chances.

In this quest for knowledge and truth,

Let us not ignore the role of subjectivity,

For it is through the combination, of objective facts and personal views,

That we can gain a more holistic and complete understanding of reality.

So let us approach the world with an open mind,

And a willingness to consider multiple perspectives,

For it is through this diversity of thought,

That we can gain a deeper and more nuanced understanding of the world and
its aspects.

In the end, let us remember, that facts are a foundation,

But they are not the only thing that shapes our understanding of the world,

It is important to consider the role of subjectivity,

To gain a more complete and holistic understanding of the world.

15. Ink & Quill: The Power and Responsibility of Writing

Verily, the art of writing doth engender

A profundity of thought and pen

For in the scribe's quill, doth lie a splendor

That doth transcend the mortal ken

With each stroke of ink, doth meaning render

To the blank page, a life of its own

A tale of woe, or joy, or splendor

That doth in the mind's eye, fully shown

But writing is not just ink and quill

It is the very breath of the soul

For in each word, doth truth distill

And in each verse, doth wisdom roll

And thus, the scribe doth hold in hand

The power to shape the mortal land

For in the written word, doth history expand

And the future doth, in ink, command

But let us not forget, dear friends

The weight of the written word

For with each thought, it doth attend

To kindle or snuff out, like a bird

So let us choose our words with care

And in each sentence, sow a seed

For in the written word, doth the future fair

And the past, in memory, be freed.

And thus, the scribe's art doth bestow

Upon the world, a lasting legacy

For in the written word, doth knowledge flow
And the truth, in ink, doth clearly see
But writing is not just for the learned
It is a skill for one and all
For in each person's heart, is a story yearned
And in each mind, a tale to call
And so, let us all take up the pen
And let our thoughts and feelings flow
For in the written word, doth the human ken
And the beauty of the world, show.
For in the written word, doth the human mind
Find solace, and understanding too
And in the written word, doth one's own kind
Find empathy, compassion, and virtue.
And so, let us embrace the art of writing
With reverence and humility
For in the written word, doth our souls be smiting
And the world, in ink, doth eternity.
But let us not forget, that writing is also a tool
For manipulation and deceit
For in the written word, doth a cleverly worded rule
For in the written word, doth a cleverly worded rule
And the truth, in ink, doth retreat
And so, let us use our words with care
And in each sentence, sow a seed of truth
For in the written word, doth power repair
And the world, in ink, doth proof.
For in the written word, doth the human voice
Find a platform, to be heard
And in the written word, doth one's own choice
Find expression, and to be preferred.

And so, let us use our power to write
With responsibility and integrity
For in the written word, doth our future take flight
And the world, in ink, doth eternity.
Let us be the scribe, the author, the poet,
That pens the story of our time
And let us use our power to show it
That together, we can make it shine.
Let us be the scribe, who doth unravel
The mysteries of the human mind
And let us be the poet, who doth travel
The depths of the heart, to find.
For in the written word, doth the human spirit
Find the courage to soar and dream
And in the written word, doth one's own merit
Find the strength to face life's scheme.
And so, let us embrace the art of writing
With passion and creativity
For in the written word, doth our souls be igniting
And the world, in ink, doth beauty.
Let us write of love, and hope, and grace
And let us write of sorrow, and pain
For in the written word, doth the human race
Find the courage to rise again.
For in the written word, doth the human soul
Find the light to guide the way
And in the written word, doth one's own goal
Find the path, to make it stay.
Let us remember
That writing is a power, and a gift
For in the written word, doth the world September

And in ink, doth the future lift.
Let us write with purpose, and with care
And let us write with intention and thought
For in the written word, doth the world repair
And in ink, doth the future be brought.
Let us write of love, and hope, and peace
And let us write of unity and kindness
For in the written word, doth the world release
From the shackles of hate and blindness.
Let us write of progress and change
And let us write of equality and justice
For in the written word, doth the world arrange
A better future, free from mistrust.
And so, let us embrace the art of writing
With reverence and responsibility
For in the written word, doth the world be exciting
And in ink, doth our destiny.
Let us be the scribe, who doth pen
The story of a better tomorrow
And let us use our power to begin
A new chapter, free from sorrow.
Let us be the scribe, who doth transcribe
The beauty of the world, in ink
And let us be the poet, who doth describe
The wonders of life, that make us think.
For in the written word, doth the human heart
Find the beauty in the ordinary
And in the written word, doth one's own part
Find the meaning, in life's journey.
And so, let us use our power to write
With compassion and understanding

For in the written word, doth the world ignite
And in ink, doth the future expanding.
Let us write of hope, and love, and dreams
And let us write of overcoming fear
For in the written word, doth the world beams
And in ink, doth the future be dear.
Let us be the scribe, who doth record
The history of the world, in ink
And let us be the poet, who doth afford
The future, a brighter, clearer think.
In conclusion, let us embrace
The art of writing with open hearts
For in the written word, doth the world face
A future, where beauty departs.
Let us embrace
The art of writing with open hearts
For in the written word, doth the world grace
A future, where beauty departs.
Let us be the scribe, who doth preserve
The memories, and the lessons of the past
And let us be the poet, who doth serve
The present and the future, that will last.
For in the written word, doth the human race
Find the wisdom to move forward
And in the written word, doth one's own pace
Find the strength to overcome the hurdle.
And so, let us use our power to write
With purpose and with determination
For in the written word, doth the world ignite
And in ink, doth the future, a new sensation.
Let us write of progress, and of change

And let us write of love and unity

For in the written word, doth the world arrange

A future, where all can thrive in harmony.

Let us remember , That writing is a powerful tool

For in the written word, doth the world is paper , And in ink, doth the future, rule.

16. Mind's Labyrinth: The Power of Thought and Intuition

In the realm of thoughts, where the mind doth roam,

A labyrinth of ideas, a cognitive dome.

A place where reason and logic do reside,

And the sparks of inspiration oft abide.

But what is this act of thinking, we inquire,

A neural process, or a mental fire?

Is it but a product of the brain,

Or something more, a cosmic gain?

Perchance, it is the essence of our being,

The very thing that sets us apart from mere seeing.

A capability that sets us apart,

From all other creatures of heart.

Thinking, a means by which we comprehend,

The nature of the world and our place in it to tend.

Through thoughts and ideas, we shape our fate,

And create a reality, that is truly great.

But as we ponder, and our thoughts do delve,

We must remember, that to think is to be delved.

For in the act of thinking, we are changed,

Our perspectives altered, rearranged.

Thus, let us think, but think with care,

For in the realm of thoughts, we are but a mere player.

Let us strive to understand, not simply to know,

And in doing so, our minds shall truly grow.

For in the end, it is not the destination,

But the journey that is the true sensation.

Let us think, and let our thoughts take flight,

For in the realm of thoughts, there is infinite might.

But with great power comes great responsibility,

For thoughts, once formed, can shape our destiny.

It is crucial to be mindful, and to reflect,

On the thoughts that guide us, and the paths they select.

For thoughts, like seeds, can blossom or wilt,

Depending on the soil in which they are built.

Let us tend to our thoughts with care,

And cultivate a garden of positivity and awareness.

For it is not only the destination that matters,

But also the journey, and how it alters and flatters.

Let us strive to think with clarity and grace,

And in doing so, we shall find our place.

So let us think, and let our thoughts soar,

For in the realm of thoughts, there is always more.

Let us use this power to create a better world,

And to realize our true potential, unfurled.

For in the end, it is not the destination,

But the journey that is the true sensation.

Let us think, and let our thoughts take flight,

For in the realm of thoughts, there is infinite might.

Yet, let us not forget the importance of stillness,

For in the midst of thoughts, true wisdom can be witness.

The art of contemplation, of introspection,

Is the key to understanding our own perception.

For thoughts, though powerful, can also deceive,

Leading us astray and making us believe.

In illusions and false truths that we create,

And the mind can easily fall prey to this fate.

But through stillness and mindfulness, we can transcend,

The noise of thoughts, and find inner peace to attend.
For in the silence, we can hear the voice of truth,
Guiding us towards our own self-proof.
So let us think, and let our thoughts run free,
But also take time for introspection and to be.
Let us use our thoughts to elevate and inspire,
And to find a balance, that will never expire.
For in the end, it is not the destination,
But the journey that is the true sensation.
Let us think, and let our thoughts take flight,
For in the realm of thoughts, there is infinite might.
Let us embrace the power of thinking,
And use it to reach for the stars, a never-ending,
Journey of self-discovery, growth and betterment,
For the mind is a powerful instrument.
But let us not forget, that thoughts are not the only way,
To connect with the world, to understand and play.
There is also intuition, a deeper knowing,
That comes from within, and is often glowing.
It is a voice that speaks, in whispers and hues,
Guiding us towards the paths that we choose.
And though it may not always be clear,
It is a voice that is always sincere.
So let us listen to both thoughts and intuition,
And allow them to work in unison.
For they both have their own unique role,
In helping us reach our ultimate goal.
Thoughts for analysis and understanding,
Intuition for guidance and expanding.
Together they can lead to true enlightenment,
And bring about a new, powerful alignment.

So let us think, and let our thoughts take flight,

But also listen to the voice of intuition, that is always right.

For in the realm of thoughts, there is infinite might,

And in the balance of thought and intuition, true wisdom takes sight.

Let us use the power of thinking,

To not only understand but to also live,

To create, to feel, to love, to give.

For the mind is a powerful instrument, let us use it wisely, to truly live.

And as we navigate the realm of thoughts,

Let us not forget the importance of empathy and compassion.

For in understanding others, we can truly see,

The interconnectedness of humanity.

Through empathy, we can bridge divides,

And break down the walls that separate our lives.

We can see the world through different eyes,

And come to realize, that in diversity, true beauty lies.

So let us think, and let our thoughts take flight,

But also open our hearts to the plight,

Of others and strive for understanding,

For it is through empathy, true peace is expanding.

As we journey through the realm of thoughts,

Let us not forget the importance of balance in all sorts.

Of thoughts, intuition, empathy, and action,

For it is through balance, true satisfaction.

So let us think, and let our thoughts take flight,

But also strive for balance and insight.

For in the realm of thoughts, there is infinite might,

And it is through balance that true wisdom takes sight.

The power of thinking is immense,

Let us use it to make sense,

Of the world around us, and within,

And strive for a better future to begin.

Special Note

Dear Reader,

Thank you for taking the time to read this book. Your interest and engagement has brought life to the pages and helped bring the story to life. It is truly a privilege to have you as a reader and we appreciate your support.

As a token of gratitude, we would like to extend our sincerest thanks for choosing to spend your valuable time with us. Your interest in this book has touched our hearts and we hope that it has inspired and enlightened you in some way.

Please know that your support means the world to us and we are so grateful for the opportunity to share our story with you. We hope that you will continue to support us in the future and that you will always find joy and satisfaction in the books you choose to read.

Once again, thank you for reading and we hope that you will keep us in mind for your next literary journey.

Warmest regards,

A Team

Note

As I, a breviloquent raptor, wield A lever, with naught else to my design, I generate tones for the aural field In this prosaic orb we call mankind. My actions, though, are but a small part Of forces far beyond my control, For nature holds the key to each chart And sets the laws that govern the whole. But still, I am compelled to explore The workings of this vast machinery, To seek the truth that lies at core And find the answers to humanity. Though some may call it quest I'll seek the truth, with no time to rest.

About The Author

Meet Mawphniang Napoleon, a man of many talents and passions. As a lawyer and entrepreneur, he has achieved success in the professional world, but his true passion lies in writing and humanism. He is a soul ever-striving, never at ease, with boundless curiosity and verve. He embraces new ideas with an open mind and ventures boldly into unknown lands. He is passionate about seeking all that life has to offer, cherishing the small things and on a journey of self-discovery. He writes his story with fearlessness and making the most of every moment, ever-unfurled. He is originally from Syadheh, Ri Bhoi District in Meghalaya, India.

P.C : Clarissa Candace Giri

www.ingramcontent.com/pod-product-compliance
Lightning Source LLC
Chambersburg PA
CBHW031259130726
47988CB00007B/2638